May 4, 1992

Dear Jane,
I hope this book will
be an encouragement to you
in the first year of your
baby's life!
Love,
Pam
Proverbs 3:5,6

THE NEW MOTHERS GUIDE

Ruth Alig & Stephanie Wright

NAVPRESS
A MINISTRY OF THE NAVIGATORS
P.O. BOX 6000, COLORADO SPRINGS, COLORADO 80934

The Navigators is an international Christian organization. Jesus Christ gave His followers the Great Commission to go and make disciples (Matthew 28:19). The aim of The Navigators is to help fulfill that commission by multiplying laborers for Christ in every nation.

NavPress is the publishing ministry of The Navigators. NavPress publications are tools to help Christians grow. Although publications alone cannot make disciples or change lives, they can help believers learn biblical discipleship, and apply what they learn to their lives and ministries.

Unless otherwise identified, Scripture quotations in this publication are from the *Holy Bible: New International Version* (NIV). Copyright © 1973, 1978, 1984, International Bible Society. Used by permission of Zondervan Bible Publishers. Another version used is the *New American Standard Bible* (NASB), © The Lockman Foundation 1960, 1962, 1963, 1968, 1971, 1972, 1973, 1975, 1977.

Printed in the United States of America

CONTENTS

We dedicate this book to our firstborn,
Asher and Zachary,
remembering them and our first year of motherhood
with thanksgiving to God.

***

Our many thanks
to our husbands, Vince and Daniel,
for their continual love and support
throughout this project;
to our parents and friends
who provided many hours of care
for our children;
to all who encouraged us
through their words and supported us
with their prayers.

The friendship of Ruthie Alig and Stephanie Wright began in the fall of 1978 during their sophomore year at college. The kinship they immediately experienced was not by chance. The Spirit of God had brought together two young women who had a mutual appreciation for literature, a desire to write, and a growing faith in Jesus Christ.

As their friendship matured, they saw a need to challenge each other to use their creative abilities, especially in writing. An Old Testament scripture became their personal theme of encouragement for one another:

"Naphtali is a doe let loose, He gives beautiful words."
Genesis 49:21, NASB

Ruthie and Stephanie know that writing a book together is a fulfillment of a hope and a dream God placed in their hearts while in college. They sincerely desire to be writers who give "beautiful words" to others—encouraging them to grow in grace and knowledge of the Lord Jesus.

They were both English majors at Salem College in

Winston-Salem, North Carolina. Ruthie also ahs a Bachelor of Arts degree in art history and a Master of Arts degree in theology from Fuller Theological Seminary. Stephanie has a Master of Arts degree in communications from Wheaton College Graduate School.

Ruthie lives in Indianapolis, Indiana, with her husband, Vince, a Presbyterian minister, and their two children, Zachary and Alisa. She is a freelance writer, and has taught classes and given presentations on sacred dance as worship.

Stephanie lives in Atlanta, Georgia, with her husband, Daniel, a manager in the hotel industry, and their son, Asher. She is a freelance writer and a consultant in public relations and marketing.

A friend in the universe is a light in the darkness.

Our names are Stephanie and Ruthie, and we are friends. We met in the fall of 1978 in college, never realizing that our friendship would grow and mature for years to come. We have been roommates, dreamers, strugglers, writers, encouragers, and forgivers for one another. We have lived as far apart as California and North Carolina, Indianapolis and Atlanta. Yet the grace of God has allowed us to remain friends through all the distance and changes. For this we are thankful.

We witnessed each other's courtship and marriage and kept in touch as our marriages matured. Then something happened that we had not dreamed of or analyzed in advance; within five months of each other, we became mothers.

In May of 1986, we spent a few days together at the beach. For the first time, we were able to share, face to face, what had been happening in our lives since we had become mothers. As we walked beside the ocean, we discovered many common experiences and a refreshing empathy for one

9

another. Through talking about both the joyous and difficult times, a mutual desire developed in our hearts to write about what we were learning. We especially wanted to explore, through research and writing, the aspects of mothering that had caught us by surprise.

So we come to you as friends, inviting you to walk on the beach with us, sharing your life as a new mother. You will discover that we still struggle with contradictions, yet rejoice in how we have grown to delight in being mothers. We do not offer a "how to be a good mother" book, nor do we even want to dictate how you should feel about mothering. Our main hope is to encourage you and to be friends who can identify with you.

Although we have been friends for years, we are not identical. Between us, we were influenced by a very traditional mother and a very untraditional mother. One of us sees herself combining a career and motherhood; the other chooses to be an "at-home" mother. We feel our differences will help keep our study balanced, for we realize that you (and all new mothers) are truly unique.

Our bond with one another and with you is our faith in Jesus Christ. We believe that a relationship with Jesus Christ is the only way to know your identity as a human, a woman, and a mother. If we can encourage you as a new mother in any way to trust Jesus, then our hopes for this book are met. Back to our beach walk. . . .

As you explore the beach at different times of the day, you realize that the ocean never washes in the same treasure or debris. The constant change encountered with each high and low tide is similar to what motherhood in the United States has experienced over the last 100 years. With each passing decade, the culture writes a new definition of motherhood—an emphatic assertion that this new pronouncement is the right and only way to mother.

So if we look at the last century of changing tides for mothers, which we challenge you to do, we vividly realize that there is only one Person to go to for our true place and identity: our Lord Jesus Christ.

While journeying through the new role of mother, you cannot look to society's mandates to determine what it means for you, personally, to be a mother. Neither can you search for your identity in the role of motherhood alone, for motherhood will become an idol. Christ *must* be your first love. Disappointment will come if you seek your self-worth and integrity from any other source.

So with words of encouragement and challenge, we continue with you as you grow in maturity as His disciple during your first year of motherhood:

> No one has arrived—we're all on a journey. We have a mutual destiny: to be conformed to the image of Christ—His image, not ours.[1]

> This is the missing step in the walk of far too many women . . . in our new day. The center of life is in one's relationship to the Lord Jesus Christ. How much one is a mirror of the Maker. How much one's lifestyle reveals the wisdom of God.[2]

NOTES:
1. Elaine Stedman, *A Woman's Worth* (Waco, Tex.: Word Books, 1980), page 40.
2. From the book *Liberated Traditionalism* by Ronald and Beverly Allen, copyright 1985 by Multnomah Press. Published by Multnomah Press, Portland, Oregon. Used by permission. Page 203.

Because of the deep and complex nature of motherhood, we have tried to create a study format that touches all dimensions of the experience in a way that will help you integrate the whole picture of motherhood from your own perspective. It is important to note that this book is focused on you as a new mother and not on your child. In our experience we found plenty of material on the development of a baby, but little on the development of a mother.

Our studies target the traditional family—wife, husband, and child. We are aware that some new mothers may not have a husband, but we have not been able to include their special needs in this book. Nor do we have sufficient room to discuss adequately the history of women's issues. We encourage you to further explore issues that especially interest or concern you. For we have come to understand that an informed, historical perspective can help us find place and identity in the present.

Throughout this study, we have given reference to many books and periodicals that will assist you in your personal research. Three excellent books that give a Christian perspective on women's issues are: *Liberated Traditionalism* by Ronald and Beverly Allen, *Women at the Crossroads* by Kari T. Malcolm, and *Women: Beyond Equal Rights* by Dee Jepsen.

We have organized the developmental information on a monthly basis, dealing with the physical and psychological dimensions of the first twelve months of motherhood.

The first section of each chapter is called "Body and Mind." This section includes the developmental information and topical discussions about modern issues related to motherhood. Since our chronological arrangement of information may not correspond exactly to your experience, feel free to choose the chapter most appropriate to your own schedule of interest and need.

Following "Body and Mind" is a section for your personal *reflection* on body, mind, and relevant issues.

Next follows "Heart and Spirit," a Bible study that corresponds with the developmental stages and topical discussions presented in "Body and Mind." We encourage you to examine the Scriptures carefully and respond to study questions.

Finally, we have a section called "Prayers and Answers." Here you can record your spiritual struggles and growth as you walk with God through each month of motherhood.

Our hopes for you, as you read and study this book, pivot around two verses:

May our Lord Jesus Christ himself and God our
Father, who loved us and by his grace gave us eternal
encouragement and good hope, encourage your hearts
and strengthen you in every good deed and word.
                              2 Thessalonians 2:16-17, NIV

We deeply hope that you will be encouraged to make your decisions about mothering under the lordship of Jesus

Christ, and that your confidence will be strengthened for the fulfillment of your role as a mother. We also hope that you will feel less isolated from others in your choices and experiences regarding motherhood. Perhaps you will want to use this book for study and fellowship as you get together with other new mothers.

When the year is done, this book will remain as a personal record of a special year of growth and change in your life.

IN THE BEGINNING

BODY AND MIND

Greetings, new mother! Welcome to the baffling, beautiful world of motherhood! Your life's journey has taken you through many experiences: a childhood of playing family, an adolescence of crushes and dreams of love, and an adulthood of discovering your identity and giving yourself to another person in marriage. But the journey has recently taken you through yet another turn in the road. For nine months you carried within your body the life of a new person. This child has begun his or her own journey now, and has caused you to become more than an adult woman; you are now a "mother."

The rules of the road have changed. All the knowledge you have gathered thus far seems incomplete as you face the task before you that is filled with unknowns.

Your introduction to the world of motherhood was not accomplished by following an easy set of instructions, but by the jarring pain of labor and delivery. Whether you are recovering in the hospital or at home, pause and try to assimilate the dramatic alterations of body and mind that you are experiencing during your first month of motherhood.

The Physical Realities

Labor and delivery is strenuous, teeth-gritting work. When the task of birthing is accomplished, your physical condition is called *puerperium*. Puerperium begins immediately following childbirth and lasts for about six weeks, during which time your body returns to its prepregnant state. During puerperium, your body undergoes major physical adjustments. The following discussion highlights some typical elements involved in this transition period.

When your child is born, you are understandably exhausted. Though you may long to sleep when they return you to your hospital room, a nervous excitement keeps you awake and wondering about all that has just happened to you. If excitement does not keep you awake, plenty of other distractions will—especially those involving your body.

As you lie in bed, the aches and pains from delivery begin to throb. The pain is not imaginary; you have a genuine reason to hurt. Your cervix, vagina, and perineum (the area of tissue between the vagina and the anus) are bruised from delivery. If you had an episiotomy (an incision made to enlarge the vaginal opening), your wound and stitches will be painful, although medication is helpful. Due to the tremendous pressure of pushing during delivery, hemorrhoids may have appeared, adding to your general discomfort in the region you sit upon.

Judith Gansberg and Arthur Mostel, M.D., authors of *The Second Nine Months*, recommend doing Kegel exercises regularly to relieve soreness from stitches and hemorrhoids. They say, "Doing Kegels regularly can enhance the blood circulation in the perineum and promote more rapid healing."[1] If Kegel exercises are unfamiliar to you, your doctor or nurse can explain exactly how to do them.

During puerperium, most women experience some problems in elimination. Excess fluids and wastes are often released through the skin, causing profuse perspiration. If you awake soaked with perspiration, ask the nurse to give you fresh sheets and a nightgown to make you more comfortable.

Urinating while sustaining a bottom full of stitches and hemorrhoids is at best awkward, and the first bowel movement can be a much-dreaded event. In addition to these difficulties, some women suffer from abdominal stitches and gas pains resulting from a Caesarean birth. With the guidance of the nurses, you can take walks, drink lots of fluids, and eat plenty of fruit and roughage to help your system return to normal.

Meanwhile, blood and tissues (called lochia) flow continually from the uterus, as in menstruation, cleansing the womb and soiling the ice packs and bed pads beneath you. The lochia will be dark red for the first two to three days. Then it turns a pinkish color for about the next seven days. Finally it becomes a creamy, yellow color and will last for another week or two. When the flow of the lochia stops, the cervix is considered completely closed.

Also during puerperium, your uterus rapidly reduces to its normal size. This process is called involution. The nurse may teach you to massage right below your navel in order to help the process of involution. You may experience uterine cramps or after-pains as a result of this rapid shrinkage of your uterus, but such pains are generally not as common after a first birth as they are after subsequent births.

Never in your life have you experienced such rapid weight loss as after delivery. On the average, a woman loses ten to twelve pounds upon delivery of the infant, placenta, and amniotic fluid. But this weight loss does not mean an immediate return to normal abdominal muscle tone. Improvement in muscle tone comes in time from a good diet and sufficient exercise, but immediately after delivery, your stomach may feel soft and spongy—like bread dough.

If you have stretch marks, or striae, you know that they were red to purple at delivery. These marks gradually fade, appearing only faintly on the skin as silver or white streaks.

In conjunction with the upheaval of childbirth, your body undergoes the most dramatic hormonal fluctuation of your life. While the level of estrogen drops sharply, the level of prolactin rises as your body prepares for lactation, or the secretion of milk. This reversal does not occur without emotional and/or physical side effects. Flowing tears and aching breasts are signs that your body is preparing to nourish your child.

These physical adjustments begin taking place in a hospital setting that may seem alien to you; many women have never been in a hospital prior to the birth of their first child. In addition to coping with these dramatic changes and new experiences, you must adapt to the schedule of the doctors and nurses. The doctors and nurses check on you regularly—examining stitches, blood pressure, temperature, and your general well-being. In your postpartum exhaustion, learning which button is for calling the nurse and which is for raising the bed can seem like an enormous task. Try to remember that the hospital staff is there to support you through puerperium, and more and more they truly do focus on the mother's total needs at this critical time, whether it be for pain relief or for encouragement that she will learn how to change a diaper.

The first two to three days after delivery have been called the "taking-in" phase.[2] During this phase you may feel passive and dependent on others as you recover physically from the effects of giving birth. You are willing to follow suggestions and do not desire to make many decisions. Eating and sleeping are high priorities, and it is difficult to do much else, except maybe think repeatedly about the delivery of your child. Once you understand your physical condition as a new mother, it should not be difficult to understand why you experience the "taking-in phase."

After the second or third day, the "taking-hold" phase clicks in, and you are ready to begin taking control of matters.[3] A shower seems like a feasible venture, and you might even feel strong enough to attempt that first bowel movement. I experienced this need to regain control about the second day and took the effort to fix my hair and apply some makeup, a task that symbolized my ability to once again become more oriented toward others. At this stage, you become more inclined to focus on learning childcare skills and become more involved in what is happening around you.

So now you have experienced and read about some of the graphic, physical realities of early motherhood. The unknowns that you tried to imagine during pregnancy have occurred and left their impression on you. Your body has worked very hard, and you are to be commended for what you have endured to give a child life. But your body has not been alone in this recovery effort; your mind is in a recovery-discovery process of its own.

Your Mind: Making Sense of the New Reality

Tick, tick, tick . . . your mind busily categorizes your daily experiences, some more exciting than others. Then, birth occurs. . . . Wow! Your mind is suddenly forced into a flurry of activity; it must quickly develop new categories to handle the flood of novel feelings associated with your new role as mother. Helene Deutsch, author of *The Psychology of Women*, writes, "It is logical to assume that an event involving greatly heightened inner tension and a tremendous physical upheaval will produce important psychic material."[4]

Remember, for a moment, what you were thinking and feeling immediately after the birth of your child. If all went well and the child was healthy, you may have felt relieved and somewhat victorious. Feeling a sense of great achievement is not unusual, because you have conquered pain and fear and brought the world fresh hope through the life of your new-born child. Awe and stillness may accompany the first sight of your child, so fragile and unfathomable. Blending into this dream-like state of joy are the more troubling thoughts of concern for your baby's health or disappointment over something related to the birth event, perhaps an unexpected Caesarean section.

When Zachary was born, the doctor exclaimed, "What a floppy baby!" My eyes wide, I asked, "What's wrong?" "Poor muscle tone," he replied. "He'll be fine." I relaxed with a sigh.

Next, they placed Zachary on the examining tray and surrounded him so I could not see him. "We'll have to take him to the special care nursery for a while because he's having some breathing difficulties," said a nurse as they wheeled him out of the room. My husband trailed after them to tell his parents that the baby had come and to watch him through the nursery window. After making sure I was all right, the last nurse left and I was alone for the next half hour, wondering what was happening.

I do not remember being very anxious, but the quiet of that room made a strong impression on my psyche. The mystery of life and death seemed very close to me in the hush of those moments. Zachary was returned to me shortly thereafter, and he has been a very healthy baby ever since.

Although some women feel heightened intimacy with their spouse after delivery, others just feel tired and may worry about their lack of enthusiasm for husband or baby. If you are a tired mother, do not feel guilty if you don't feel like doing handsprings around the delivery room or giving your husband a big hug. Your time of joy will come after you have the rest you so desperately need.

A new mother's thoughts and emotions will probably remain jumbled for a while. Your mind is working hard to assimilate all the data related to your experience. Soon you will emerge from the confusion and continue on your journey into motherhood with a marvelous ability to reflect on those first moments of being a mother.

When your baby is placed in your arms, your relationship begins face-to-face—mother and child. You have so much to discover about this little person, who may now seem more like a stranger than you had ever imagined possible. And he or she has much to learn about you! You both have begun a marvelous adventure of personal interaction that will evolve through the coming years as you change and grow.

Meanwhile, you attempt to tell the good news to your family and friends and receive the visits of well-wishers. Your supportive network becomes aware that a baby has arrived and that you have inherited a new role—one that will impact your relationship with all of them. You may find yourself especially eager to share the news with your own mother and may find that your relationship to her is very important to you at this time (more on mothers and daughters in Chapter Four). All this social interaction may exhaust you, but you are compelled by the joyous quality of the news to expend the emotional energy anyway.

If you are like many women today, you became a mother with little or no previous experience in infant care. Thus, the hospital is your training ground for learning an abundance of skills. The nurses teach you how to bathe, diaper, burp, and hold the baby. Learning how to feed your baby, especially for the nursing mother, is an absorbing task. You also learn how to care for the umbilical cord, and for little boys, you learn circumcision care. The pediatrician visits you in the hospital and gives you lots of information regarding your child. After a few days of this intensive training, you leave the hospital with your baby. As the nurse waves goodbye, you wonder why you do not feel exactly confident about what lies ahead.

Once home, your body continues to remind you that you have been through something serious. Stitches throb and you are exhausted. Breasts ache and flab seems to cling to you mercilessly. Your days are filled with the heat lamp, sitz bath, and sanitary napkin routine. You would like to crawl into bed and not be disturbed for a month, but your baby's cry draws you to respond time and time again.

These days are a time of great physical weakness accompanied by great physical exertion. You care for the child in spite of how you feel, and your maternal instinct goes through a trial by fire. You want the child to survive, but you wonder if *you* will survive. The psychological reaction to this paradoxical period of weakness and exertion varies for each woman, but feelings of inadequacy and depression are common (more on depression in Chapter Two).

Much has happened to you in the first month of motherhood, both physically and psychologically. Perhaps you think the difficulties have been emphasized more than the joys. But if the discussion seems unbalanced, it is only because the quantity of adjustments made during this first month creates this picture. Your joys during this time are very real too, and they play a major role in helping you recover. Savor your joys, and watch them grow in depth and strength as this year unfolds.

You have had a unique experience in giving birth—so unique that this book could never account for all you have felt and thought. But many mothers have known similar experiences, so you need not feel entirely alone on this journey.

————————| REFLECTIONS |————————

Describe three surprises, or unexpected feelings and experiences, you've had during this first month of motherhood.

Write a brief, personal response to each of the experiences listed below.

- The birth of your child:

• Holding your child for the first time:

• Your hospital stay:

What has been the most difficult adjustment for you this month?

What has been your greatest joy as a new mother?

────────────────┤ HEART AND SPIRIT ├────────────────

1. Read Genesis 1:1-2 and write it out in the space below. Study it carefully, making notes in the margin.

2. God created the heavens and the earth.

   a. How do you see Him continuing to create through you in the birth of your child?

   b. What purpose do you understand God to have in the creation of human life?

3. You are "in the beginning" of a whole new creation—new mother, new father, new baby, new family. We have discussed the physical and psychological changes resulting from this new creation. What spiritual changes are occurring within you?

4. Before conception, the interior of your womb was dark and held no form. But out of this void God created life. Just as God created your child through a process, from darkness to life, so will He give your motherhood form and meaning. In what ways do you feel in darkness about mothering?

5. Read and write down John 1:1-5.

6. Through whom does Scripture say all of creation was made?

Thus, Christ intimately understands your role in creation.

7. Jesus is the light who shines in the darkness. What specific ways do you need Him to help you with your uncertainties about motherhood?

8. Jesus is with you in the beginning of your journey into motherhood. Talk to Him in prayer, read of Him in Scripture, and share your burdens and joys with other women who know Him.

   a. What discoveries have you made about motherhood so far?

   b. How has Christ been at work in your life at this time?

For further meditation, see Colossians 1:15-20.

| PRAYERS AND ANSWERS |

Give thanks for the safe delivery of your child and the healing taking place in your body.

Share your uncertainties and fears with the Lord, and seek His comfort.

Pray for other women who were/are in the hospital with you. Pray specifically for their recovery and strengthening for the care of their babies.

Write down any prayer requests that you have concerning motherhood.

"A mother's is the most intimate, willing, and dependable of all services, because it is the truest of all. None has been able to fulfill it properly but Christ, and He alone can."

Julian of Norwich, 1373

NOTES:
1. Judith Gansberg and Arthur Mostel, M.D., *The Second Nine Months* (New York: Tribeca, 1984), page 134.
2. Sally Olds, et al., *Maternal Newborn Nursing* (Menlo Park, Calif.: Addison-Wesley, 1988), page 1086.
3. Olds, *Maternal Newborn Nursing*.
4. Helene Deutsch, *The Psychology of Women* (New York: Bantam Books, 1945), page 219.

JOY AND ANGUISH

Four weeks or more have passed since the birth of your child, yet your physical healing may still be incomplete. The groin area may still be sensitive due to the episiotomy or hemorrhoids, or both. Breast soreness is common at this stage for nursing mothers; problems can arise due to infections or blocked milk ducts, but often, the nipples just hurt from the infant's sucking.

The uterus should have contracted back to its normal size by now, although there may still be some lochia. Your abdominal muscle tone is not yet fully restored. Perhaps you are contending with persistent extra pounds that are not dropping off as rapidly as you may wish, especially if you are nursing. (The nursing mother has to increase her caloric intake in order to sustain milk production and sufficient energy. So the foods she eats should be of excellent nutritional value.)

The primary physical detriment of this period is most often your loss of sleep. The adjustment to an interrupted

31

sleep pattern is difficult. As a result, exhaustion permeates every dimension of your being; your body craves sleep. For the sake of your health, you must rest whenever possible, even if it means abandoning household duties or other obligations.

During this month you will probably go for your postpartum checkup. At this time the nurse will record your weight and measure your blood pressure. The doctor will examine your breasts and make an internal examination to observe the healing of your episiotomy, uterus, ovaries, and vagina. He or she will also discuss your resumption of birth control methods (if you choose to use them). The doctor should advise you concerning the reestablishment of sexual intercourse with your husband and help you understand how to best handle the adjustment (see Chapter Three for a more thorough discussion of sexuality). Be sure to ask the doctor about any questions or concerns you have about these or other changes.

You are still very new at mothering, and perhaps by now the seeds of early, vague questions and problems have blossomed into more visible forms. The psychological portrait of a two-month-old mother is impossible to paint accurately because women differ in so many ways. However, because of its prevalence among new mothers, postpartum blues is a relevant discussion topic for most women.

Understanding the New-Mother Blues

You may have experienced the worst of the blues during the first month, but for some women depression occurs during the second month. Gansberg and Mostel, in their book *The Second Nine Months*, remark that an estimated eighty percent of all women have experienced postpartum depression, or what they call "an adjustment disorder."[1] The textbook *Obstetric Nursing* reads as follows:

The "postpartum blues" are a transient period of depression occurring during the puerperium. It may be manifested by anorexia, tearfulness, difficulty in sleeping, and a "letdown" feeling. . . . Ego adjustment and hormonal changes are both thought to be causal factors, although fatigue, discomfort, stimulation overload, or stimulation deprivation may also play a part. The mother requires reassurance that these feelings are normal and an explanation as to why they occur. A therapeutic environment that permits the mother to cry without feelings of guilt is vital.[2]

When examining the causes of postpartum depression, remember the enormity of your physical depletion and how closely your body and mind are related. Besides the actual pain that drains you emotionally, you are facing a dramatic loss of sleep, which is known to be a disorienting, mood-altering factor.

Then, of course, there is your figure. You may feel depressed by your reflection in the mirror or your inability to wear anything but oversized clothes. Your psychological state is closely related to your physical image during these weeks.

But other, deeper than physical, factors are provoking the blues, too. Any sentimental ideas you had about mothers and babies are challenged by the reality you are experiencing. I remember telling my grandmother about my shocking discovery that taking care of a baby is just plain hard work. She laughed heartily at my pronouncement! Raised in a family of seven children, at a time when conveniences were scarce, she was amused that I ever thought childcare would be simple. In the beginning, I had to give up many of my romantic dreams of mothering in order to do the job and find out the true motivation for mothering.

Dealing with Depression

Motherhood can be very complicated, and the stress of adapting to its new demands has to be released, often through tears or anger.

> I heard the cry in my sleep and my whole being winced in response. Through the darkness, my tired eyes gradually focused on the digital clock, where glowing numbers revealed the hour—4:00 a.m. My husband slept soundly, not even hearing the cries. Lonely, I struggled out of bed and trudged to the nursery.
>
> Suddenly, my emotions snapped. I could not walk the next few steps to the crib where my infant son lay crying. My arms, designed to cradle him, felt heavy and useless. I collapsed on the bed in the nursery and sobbed uncontrollably. All the dark emotions that had been swirling within me during these first two weeks of motherhood came pouring out in tears. My son and I were crying in the darkness of the nursery, each hoping for help.

The paragraphs above describe my personal experience with depression that began about two weeks after Zachary was born. I know now that I was not strange or dangerous because of such feelings, but at the time I was really scared by my erratic emotions.

In *The Psychology of Women*, Helene Deutsch lists some psychological difficulties new mothers face.[3] Which concerns are yours? What others would you add to the list?

- Fear of losing your personality in favor of the child's.
- Threatened erotic values and physical beauty.
- Fear of real obligations and restrictions.
- Fear of loss of professional and intellectual values.

• Feeling of insufficiency with regard to great emotional demands of motherhood.

The blues can be quite intense, but for most women the depression begins to fade as their physical health returns, their confidence builds, and they grow more attached to the child. Also, talking to other mothers who express similar feelings seems to help relieve the guilt about being depressed. If the depression persists in severe form for a long time, professional counseling may be needed.

The work of mothering involves long hours; the tasks are multitudinous. Every day brings an abundance of new skills to learn and fears to overcome. The anguish is great, but the joy of mothering—the peaceful moments spent cradling your child, a response to your love that you see in the baby's eyes or hear in his or her gurgles—sustains you during the rough times. Each day you are gaining strength and knowledge for the long haul of being a mother. Perhaps you have even caught a glimpse of the future and realized how brief and dear these days of early infancy truly are.

As Sheila Kitzinger says in her book *Women as Mothers*, "Learning how to be a mother is not a matter of adopting a certain set of attitudes, but of expressing one's own personality in the task of responding flexibly to the child's needs. Each woman brings a unique combination of skills and experience to motherhood."[4]

| REFLECTIONS |

If you have, or had, postpartum blues, describe your feelings and actions.

What and/or who helps you keep going when you experience depression?

List three new skills you have learned and congratulate yourself on their accomplishment.

Describe an experience this month that gave you encouragement and joy.

──────────────────┤ HEART AND SPIRIT ├──────────────────

1. Read John 16:17-24. Write verse 21 in your own words.

Jesus is preparing His disciples for the pain they will feel when He leaves them. He does so by describing the pain of a woman giving birth to a child. But He also tells them that the pain will not last. They will know joy when He returns, even as a mother knows joy because of her child.

Perhaps as a new mother you have gained insight into Jesus' teaching through this illustration of childbirth's joy and anguish. If so, write your thoughts here.

2. Even in this second month your body may bear some of the scars of childbirth. You probably have not forgotten that delivering a child really hurts. Why do you think Scripture says, "She forgets the anguish"?

3. Interpreting the original Greek text, Leon Morris writes:

It may be significant that He does not speak of their sorrow being replaced by joy, but of turning into it [joy]. . . . In childbirth it is one and the same thing which is first a source of pain, then of joy.[5]

a. Do you see a transition from pain to joy in your experience of motherhood?

b. What joys have you known this month as a mother?

c. What does joy mean to you?

4. Allowing yourself to heal and gradually learn about mothering is a kindness to yourself. In what ways are you expecting too much of yourself at this time?

5. Read and then write out 2 Corinthians 12:9.

6. How are you weak at this time?

7. The power of God "is made perfect in weakness." How are you trusting God to work through your weakness?

8. Your husband, relatives, and friends may be helping you with housekeeping and other tasks. Is it difficult for you to humbly accept their help while you are still weak?

9. How do you see God's grace at work in your life?

─────────────┤ PRAYERS AND ANSWERS ├─────────────

Pray for strength for yourself and other new mothers to make it through the blues.

Ask the Holy Spirit to love your child through you, as you experience the limitations of your ability to give constantly of yourself.

Remember before God the blessing of your child.

"He tends his flock like a shepherd: He gathers the lambs in his arms and carries them close to his heart; he gently leads those that have young."

Isaiah 40:11

NOTES:
1. Judith Gansberg and Arthur Mostel, *The Second Nine Months* (New York: Tribeca, 1984), page 157.
2. Sally Olds, et al., *Obstetric Nursing* (Menlo Park, Calif.: Addison-Wesley, 1980), page 922.
3. Helene Deutsch, *The Psychology of Women, Volume II—Motherhood* (New York: Bantam Books, 1945), page 280.
4. Sheila Kitzinger, *Women as Mothers: How They See Themselves in Different Cultures* (New York: Random House, 1978), page 178.
5. Leon Morris, *The Gospel According to John* (Grand Rapids: Eerdmans Publishing Co., 1971), page 705.

HUSBAND AND WIFE— ONE FLESH

BODY AND MIND

The birth of your child ushers you and your husband into a new dimension of marriage. Not only are you adjusting to your roles as parents, you are experiencing new challenges to your intimacy.

Newlyweds, as described by Mike Mason in *The Mystery of Marriage*, "are one flesh, and they need to learn to think and to walk that way. Little wonder that the world of a new marriage is every bit as strange as the world of a newborn baby! The couple too has a brand new body to get used to—and a two-headed, four-footed body at that!"[1]

No longer newlyweds, you and your husband have your oneness to maintain as a couple, as you care for the gift of your oneness—your child. Just as your newborn is struggling to learn about his or her body and new home, you and your husband may encounter struggles in adapting to your physical condition and a changed home environment.

When Stephanie and I disclosed to each other how troubling our early experiences of sex after childbirth had

41

been, we felt greatly relieved to discover that we were not necessarily abnormal. For us, our sexuality had disturbed us deeply as new mothers; thus we felt it important to include this topic. Perhaps you will want to study this chapter with your husband.

I have relied heavily on Gansberg and Mostel's *The Second Nine Months: The Sexual and Emotional Concerns of the New Mother* for the information in this chapter. I urge you to view this chapter as an introduction to postpartum sexual concerns, not as a complete handbook on the topic. Please seek out further guidance, literature, or professional help if you still have questions after reading this chapter.

Doctors usually recommend that a couple abstain from sexual intercourse during the first six weeks after childbirth. As you know, a great amount of healing and adjustment goes on during this time, and by the end of six weeks the risk of infection is very low. So, after a positive six weeks' checkup, you're free to renew your sexual relationship with your husband. Or are you?

I'm not totally naive. During the last months of pregnancy, I suspected that I was not going to be as excited as a newlywed about sex for a while, but I really did not anticipate the physical and emotional turmoil that occurred around my third month of motherhood. In desperation I searched for a book that would explain what was going on. The doctor had warned me that intercourse might be uncomfortable for a few weeks, but he did not tell me that I might wish never to have sex again!

Fortunately, I found some books and some peace of mind. I began to understand the "whys" behind my physical and psychological loss of sex drive, and I stopped fearing that I was sexually dead forever. So I will attempt to distill for you the information that helped me ease up on the guilt and frustration as I reestablished intimacy with my husband.

Physical Obstacles

For many women, intercourse remains painful beyond the six weeks' checkup. This is especially true for nursing mothers. While nursing, a woman's level of the hormone prolactin is elevated, which decreases vaginal lubrication, making intercourse less comfortable.

Fatigue plays a crucial role in the loss of sex drive, too. Day and night you are on call, helping your baby and handling whatever else you can at home, work, or both. Sex is a really low priority when you can barely keep your eyes open. For the nursing mother, exhaustion may be more of a problem because her body exerts extra energy to convert food to milk. Other possible side effects of nursing that may hinder sexual response include: engorgement, soreness, infections, and abscesses.

Your body is not the only factor when it comes to sexual response. Your mind and emotions play a crucial role, too.

Psychological Barriers

Fear of pain is a psychological reaction to a physical reality that quickly deadens desire. This fear can lead to guilt as you say "no" to your husband night after night.

The fear of becoming pregnant again, either conscious or unconscious, may deter you from having intercourse. Deutsch notes, "Naturally, the justified fear of undesired pregnancy must not be termed pathologic but it can produce the effect of a direct inhibition."[2]

You may experience guilt regarding your husband. You are highly vulnerable to guilt in your exhausted state, and you may feel like a failure sexually. You know that your husband has needs, and you want to be with him in your heart, but your body and emotions say "no way."

You may also feel guilty about your sense of fulfillment in providing for the baby. You are intensely involved on an emotional level with your baby. Thus you may find yourself unable to give of yourself any further—even when it comes to regaining intimacy with your spouse.

It is also possible that you are confused about how to mesh your mothering and sex-partner roles. If you had any hidden beliefs that being a good mother and being sexual do not mix, they will not stay hidden for long.

You may find yourself competing with your baby for your husband's attention. I remember days when my husband would come home and be extremely excited about seeing the baby. I resented his words of greeting, "Where's Zachary?" I was insecure and wanted to be the center of attention; I was scared that by becoming a mother I had lost the number-one place in my husband's heart.

You and your husband must also deal with the changes in your physical appearance. After three months, I was still looking very maternal, with a buxom, bulging build, especially in my own mental image. *No sexy woman on television looks like me, so I must not be very attractive*, I thought.

Another element that affects your sexual relationship is the loss of spontaneity. The baby's schedule now determines your free time, and at nap time you may be ready to sleep, too. With the presence of a child in your lives, you and your husband will need to be creative as you plan time to be together.

Nursing and Sexuality
Gansberg and Mostel devote an entire chapter of their book to "Sex and the Nursing Mother." If you are nursing, how is the experience affecting you sexually?

For some mothers, the baby's sucking at the breast causes sexual arousal. The feelings are natural; they are part of the nurturing bond between you and your infant. They are not a cause for alarm or guilt.

If you are a nursing mother, you may also feel unusual about your body being used as a source of food for another person. This new experience may cause you to feel alienated from your body, thus making it more difficult to respond fully to your husband.

But you are not alone in reacting to breast-feeding. Your husband has his own response to it, which influences your sexual relationship, too. For instance, he may be uneasy with the intimacy between you and the baby as you nurse. He may not react positively to leaking breasts or the bra you sleep in.

Making Necessary Adjustments

The obstacles to your sexual adjustment may seem too many to overcome. Yet if you and your husband communicate your feelings and needs to one another, you may find that sharing in this crisis together enriches your intimacy.

Our culture places pressure on a couple to have an ideal sex life. As you enter motherhood and see this ideal failing, you may resent motherhood or blame yourself for not being a sex goddess. But Scripture turns our culture upside down and reminds us that a mature, loving relationship is not based on sex alone. The birth of your child has challenged your newlywed concepts of sex. Now you have the opportunity to trust and give to one another as you discover how to share yourselves as husband, wife, and parents.

―――――――――――― | REFLECTIONS | ――――――――――――

Has reestablishing intimacy with your husband been a struggle? If so, what obstacles have been difficult to overcome?

Are you able to share your feelings about your present sexuality with your husband? Write a brief paragraph to him describing your inner feelings at this time. Give it to him when you feel ready.

What do you observe about your husband as he adjusts to your new role as mother?

In what way does he need encouragement and sensitivity?

What positive, nonsexual experiences have you shared in these early months of parenthood?

We have focused exclusively on sexuality this month, but what else has been going on in your life this month? Record three memories.

───────────────┤ HEART AND SPIRIT ├───────────────

The book of Ephesians, in general, was written to encourage the unity of the Church. The author also chose to encourage the unity of husband and wife as a good purpose for marriage, and also as a picture of the Church.

1. Read Ephesians 5:25-33. How many times is the word *love* used?

2. What description of love is found in verse 25?

3. How is a husband to love his wife according to verse 28?

4. Read Mark 12:30-31 and then compare it to Ephesians 5:28-30. What is similar about these two passages?

5. You and your husband are the closest of neighbors. In truth, you are "one flesh." As special neighbors, you are called by Christ to love one another as you love yourselves. Describe three ways you and your husband can love one another in this manner, as you adjust both physically and psychologically to parenthood.

6. Although the temporary abstinence after childbirth may be difficult, it can be a time to develop other dimensions of love in your relationship. Read 1 Corinthians 7:4-5 and list two qualities you learned to appreciate about each other during this necessary time of abstinence.

God loves you and your husband, and as His creation marriage is a wonderful, mysterious reflection of the intimate love He wishes to share with the Church.

God's love can sustain you as you cultivate ways to help each other through the changes in these early months. In time you will become fully sexual again, and your intimacy will be all the more rich since you have weathered the crisis of birth and enjoyed the sweet taste of parenthood.

PRAYERS AND ANSWERS

Ask for God's healing to take place if you have known guilt, anger, or frustration this month regarding your sexuality.

Pray for your husband's needs and your needs as a couple.

Offer praise to God for the gift of oneness with your husband, your closest neighbor.

Pray for your child as he or she learns about love and communication through the example of you and your husband.

Pray that troubled marriages will become places of reconciliation.

Pray for new mothers whose husbands are not Christians.

"Here it is the marriage relationship, in which a man and a woman realize that oneness which belongs to their God-given nature. They 'become one flesh,' one personality. 'Flesh' means more than the physical side of life; it is the medium through which the whole personality communicates its varied emotions, longings, joys, and fears."

R. Davidson
*Genesis 1-11: The Cambridge
Bible Commentary on the
New English Bible*

NOTES:
1. Mike Mason, *The Mystery of Marriage* (Portland, Oreg.: Multnomah Press, 1985), page 131.
2. Helene Deutsch, *The Psychology of Women* (New York: Bantam Books, 1945), page 100.

FROM GENERATION TO GENERATION

Month four brings a transition in your role as a mother. You are beginning to feel like your "old self" again. Most physical aspects of giving birth have healed. Your figure is returning to normal. If you are nursing, you have established a routine. You still may have some vaginal sensitivity and find yourself tired, but all in all, you know you're gaining control over your new life.

Starting with this chapter, we will say less about your body and much more about your mind, heart, and spirit. By this change of emphasis, however, we do not mean you should ignore your body. But since the healing process has restored your physical self, your focus will be more on your inward being.

During the quiet, undisturbed moments of your day, realizations and questions about mothering start to replace the mental and emotional cloudiness you have probably felt for the last three months. Let's focus on several of those realizations.

51

The Realization of Motherhood

Since you feel physically normal again, a "now-or-never" anxiousness may rise within you. You may sense an urgency to return to the activities you enjoyed prior to becoming a mother. This impulse usually results from both a need and a fear. You have a strong need to focus on your personal interests, and a fear that unless you get involved immediately, you never will.

Another stark realization has probably punched its way through the fog: Motherhood is not always full of joy and pleasure. You have days when you want to abandon your role as mother. Boredom, mundane routines, and tiredness follow you like a shadow.

It's important to recognize that these negative thoughts and feelings are normal and will occur again. Do not condemn yourself during the difficult moments of mothering. The Lord is not your accuser. He understands the physical taxation and stress you are enduring as you grow in your new role. He understands well the trials and sacrifices involved in becoming a servant to others.

Mixed with the spurts of negativism, you also may have noticed insecurities that make you feel uneasy or inadequate as a mother. As Sheila Kitzinger points out in her book *Women as Mothers*, this, too, is normal: "The birth of the first child is almost invariably a crisis for the parents in terms of their own emotions and their sense of the enormous challenge they face."[1]

Some women, Kitzinger explains, feel insecure because they cannot predict or anticipate their child's behavior. Mothering is unlike the tasks you may have performed in the past, tasks in which all seemed orderly and certain. If mothering followed a consistent set of rules and procedures, some mothers would feel more at ease.

Another reason for insecurity may be a lack of necessary support systems to help you with your personal needs. You may be all alone with your child each day. You may have no one to assist you during stressful times. And more than likely, your child's grandparents are geographically distant.

To place this realization in its proper perspective, and to discover what we as new Christian mothers can do about this lack of support, we must recognize how impoverished motherhood has become in our society.

In our technological society, where families move from city to city and state to state every few years, we "are bereft of the traditional baby wisdom which was once transmitted through grandparents."[2] We now find ourselves "adrift in a sea of conflicting advice from experts, from neighbors, and even from a vocal faction of women . . . who decry the 'slavery' of motherhood."[3]

Dr. T. Berry Brazelton, the author of popular childcare books, voices the same concern. He asks,

> How can we raise children by the principle of "do what feels right" if we don't know where we're headed? With the breakdown of the extended family and the disintegration of our cultural values, today's parents are working in a vacuum. We have lost the kind of instinct that is directed by a culture or by an extended family, and unfortunately, there's nothing to replace it yet.[4]

Our generation has had to turn to professionals for the answers to motherhood and parenting. Because it does not come naturally to us, we "prepare for it as if we were required to operate some mysterious piece of machinery, as if we had to pass a competency test."[5] Ask yourself if you are walking a path similar to that which Anita Shreve has followed in becoming a mother:

Like many of my generation, I was not exposed to the
intimacies of child-rearing. I had never changed a
diaper, given a bath or fed a baby a bottle until I had
my own child. When I discovered I was pregnant, I
assumed that child-rearing, like childbearing, would
wondrously reveal itself when the time came. But then
I had a baby and I realized I didn't have the faintest idea
what to do with her. . . . My daughter is five now, and
for all of her life, I have been trying to learn how to be
a mother. I pay attention to what the experts say; I
compare notes with other mothers and fathers. I have a
childcare library three feet long. I have had to learn to
be a parent in the only way I know how—not by
instinct, but by the book; not as second nature, but as
a career.[6]

REFLECTIONS: THE REALIZATIONS

Before we continue with the questions about motherhood,
think about the realizations we have mentioned here. Which
ones have encircled you?

Are there any others? If so, what are they?

What anxieties and insecurities have crept into your mind
and emotions during the last four months?

In what ways do you feel impoverished as a mother?

Do you find yourself identifying with Anita Shreve? If so, in what ways and why?

The Central Questions of Motherhood

Now we shift to the second focus of this chapter: questions that may have surfaced since you became a mother. We will look at three central questions in depth for the remainder of your first year as a mother:

1. Who am I now?
2. Am I called to be a mother?
3. How will my closest relationships be affected?

We will begin developing an answer for the first question in this chapter and add new dimensions to it in Chapters Six and Seven. Question 2 will be the theme of Chapter Five. And question 3 will revolve around three relationships: your husband (Chapters Three and Eleven), your friends (Chapter Eight), and lastly, your relatives (Chapter Four).

While you ponder the questions and shape your own answers, use Matthew 11:20-29 as the foundation on which to lay your insights and developments as a new mother:

> "Come to me, all you who are weary and burdened, and I will give you rest. Take my yoke upon you and learn from me, for I am gentle and humble in heart, and you will find rest for your souls. For my yoke is easy and my burden is light."

Frequently ask yourself as you contemplate your answers to these questions, "In my new role as a mother, whose yoke am I wearing—the yoke of Jesus, or the yoke of my generation's social and cultural demands?"

Who Am I Now?

Can there be a more charged question than who am I now? Realistically, you are still you, with one more role to juggle into your already full life. Or are you the same you? Somehow this new title of mother just doesn't sound quite right to your ears as you repeat it over and over to yourself.

I recall clearly the day this title became personal. Only several hours after Asher was born, I asked myself, "Who am I now?" My thoughts and emotions were odd to me. The books I read had only hypothetically prepared me for this new role. In the middle of the muddle of my strange feelings, in my very core, I was still "me." Becoming a mom didn't change who I uniquely was, but only added a novel dimension to the old me.

When my mother arrived at the hospital that same day, I felt the same strangeness engulf me again. Now the daughter was looking at her mother as a mother. I was uncertain how this new mother role was going to merge with the old daughter role.

Think for a moment about your own experiences during the last few months. How do you see yourself as a mother, yet still a daughter? Do you find yourself asking, "What is my true identity? Who am I really?"

As you think about your unique life blueprint and the many roles drawn on it, remember Christ Jesus highly regards you as an individual human being. Know that your worth is not based upon any of your numerous roles, but on wearing His yoke, having His brand seared on your heart and mind. Keep this in mind as you finish this month's journey and proceed through the next two chapters.

For the rest of this chapter, we need to step inside a complex relationship. Side by side stand two generations: you and your mother. An invisible cord now connects the two generations. Psychologically, an interweaving has taken place since you became her colleague in her profession. You and your mother share a commonality and closeness through the mutual experience of being mothers.

During these early months of your new profession, this cord has become taut. This strong tug is more than likely your grip. Most women have a deep need for their own mother or a mother substitute during the period following childbirth.

Mothers once were asked to be present at their daughters' deliveries. Mothers shared the expectations of their daughters and ushered them into their first responsibilities as new mothers. Since this practice is rare today, sometime in the beginning months of motherhood, daughters need to be "mothered."

You are prepared emotionally for motherhood through the mothering you receive from your mother, or substitute. She becomes a mentor to you. And by reinforcing your position as a daughter who receives love, she can help establish your role as a giver of love to your child.

In recognizing your inner need to be mothered, you also see clearly that your mother permeates every aspect of your life—maybe more than you imagined she would. This unblurred sight reveals the second dimension of the two generations meeting on common ground.

Iron begins to sharpen iron. The unhewn edges from the past, in your relationship with your mother, start rubbing together. Your first impulse may be to ignore the sparks. As a new mother, creating a justifiable excuse won't be difficult, "I'm too tired to think about those unresolved conflicts and problems. My baby still requires all of my energy. Maybe in a few months I'll consider dealing with them."

Yet I believe our Lord doesn't want you to run from the fire. Instead He desires to use this clashing of generations as part of the refining process in making you into His holy likeness. He wants you to reconcile any differences, minor or major, that have wedged between you and your mother over the years.

For each of us as a new mother, the route to reconciliation will be different. But a common map of directions, telling us where our road begins, does exist.

We all must search our hearts to see what hidden hurts we have stored away. Then we need to give to our Father these minor bruises or major wounds. Through this giving over we acknowledge that we need His grace to forgive our mothers and to bring wholeness to the relationship. As we look directly at our hurts, asking the Father for wisdom, we can begin to understand why the conflicts even occurred.

At least three possible answers to "why" exist. First and foremost, our mothers are not perfect, and neither are we. Second, due to their imperfections, we may have encountered difficulties during our developmental years. Third, the social standards of our mothers' generation may have affected how they raised us. Let's briefly look at these possible reasons for the conflicts.

In the very core of your soul, where your spirit resides, are the experiences of your life from birth to now. At the bedrock is the nurturing your mother did or did not give you. Your spirit as a baby and young child recorded more than you could have mentally known at such a young age. Without consciously knowing it, the first close embraces with your mother built the foundation of your sense of personal worth and courage to mature.

Because of the inevitable modeling relationship that

occurs between a mother and daughter, your mother was the essential person to communicate trust and security to you in the early days of your life. Through warm, affectionate touching and holding, your spirit was called forth to fullness. But if consistent love and discipline were insufficient early in life, or if you were damaged by abuse, your spirit and mind may have been bruised or crippled in some part of your personal growth.[7]

As a daughter, you not only have this bond of trust, or absence of it, in your memory, but also the image of your mother as a woman and a mother. And when you became a mom a few months ago, you began fulfilling this image: who a mother is, what a mother does, and how a mother acts.

This model, now being expressed as you mother your child, was established in part during your formative years as you internalized your own mother's values and behavior. But you may find yourself either completely or partially rejecting this image.

You see what you lacked as a child. Possibly your real mom was seldom or never around. For whatever reason, a surrogate mother raised you. Your pain is abandonment. You don't want to make the same mistakes with your child that your mother made with you.

Maybe you remember her style of mothering as too confining and restricting. Maybe you just want to be yourself and not a clone of your mother's style of raising a child. Or you appreciate her concern and interest, and you desire to go to her when you need advice; yet you don't want her to always initiate recommendations on the how-tos of childcare.

Now take a moment to consider the era in history when your mother was a new mother. What was society like then? What messages did the media direct toward young mothers? What was your mother like as a young mother? What was she doing? How was she perceived by her peers? Was she working outside the home? Involved in volunteer work? Or possibly committed only to her home and family?

In reflecting on my mother's generation, I was a product of the baby boom, born in the late 1950s. Most of the moms in the neighborhood where I lived held the positions of full-time mothers and housewives. But I recall one particular mother who worked and had surrogate care for her children. Even though I was young, I sensed an air of disapproval, no support among the "non-working" mothers. One mom would not let her daughter play at this home.

I chuckle as I remember television's portrayal of the perfect mother—a "Mrs. Cleaver." My most vivid memory is Beaver's mother in the kitchen, preparing dinner. Every hair on her head was in place. She had on a spotless, wrinkle-free dress, a string of pearls around her neck, an apron around her waist, and of course wore nylons and high heels. To make this perfect-mother image complete, her face displayed a perpetual smile.

The commercials assisted in promoting this same image of the perfect mother. Again, I remember the mother in the kitchen and dressed in a similar "Mrs. Cleaver" costume. She was either cooking or mopping the linoleum floors. And that same "all-is-wonderful" smile adorned her face.

I know now, and I am sure you do too, all was not smiles—just perfect—at home. Your mother heard many voices clamoring for her attention, each one bellowing its current definition of mother.

Just as you and I cannot always discern the falsehood in our society's current proclamations, neither could your mother. She, too, may have been lured by the pearls, unaware they were counterfeit, and placed them around her neck, trying to be a mother she was not.

This deception and ignorance may be one of the sparks in your relationship. Your unresolved conflicts may come from not agreeing on a correct definition of or role for a mother—what a mother does and does not do. Realize you each have your own tainted concepts of mothering because of society's negative influences.

Thus, in understanding and analyzing any conflicts you have had with your mother, you need to remember two crucial points. First, the problems resurfacing result from how she communicated to you, and from her own imperfections. Second, society had a major affect on her personal ideas about mothering.

─────────── REFLECTIONS: THE QUESTIONS ───────────

We have just given possible reasons as to why the unresolved conflicts with your mother have found daylight again since the birth of your first child. Now you need to thoughtfully consider the specifics of your unique situation.

Ask God to begin revealing the painful areas of unresolved differences that at this point you may recall only vaguely. As you pray and listen, write down the areas where the nurturing of your own mother was incomplete, interrupted, or unsatisfying.

Do your hurts from the past revolve around possible abuse, neglect, or the absence of your natural mom?

What did you dislike about your mother's style of childraising that you now may want to reject?

Could you possibly have made an unspoken, but solemn vow never to be like your mother?

Think of mothers you know who have been beleaguered by their unresolved past as they try to merge two generation's ideas and standards of mothering. What do their struggles have in common with your own?

What attributes in your mother's values and in her methods of childraising do you wish to implement as you mother your child?

And lastly, how are you beginning to answer the question Who am I now?

In defining who you are, have you put on a prescribed yoke of today's society? Are you allowing yourself as a mother to be pulled by the constant value changes rather than being guided by the loving pull of our Lord's yoke? Write down the ways you see yourself being controlled by the yoke of today's standards.

─────────────┤ HEART AND SPIRIT ├─────────────

You have looked at some realizations about mothering and questions that have been forming over the last four months. In this section, you will go a step further with the question Who am I now? You need to define who you are today in relation to your mother and who you want to be.

As we previously discussed, a major part of yourself is tied to the past with your mother. You've also been thinking about the conflicts and pains from your past. They may be only minor scratches, or they may be serious gashes of physical, mental, or emotional abuse.

No matter what your personal situation is, a process of healing and becoming whole needs to take place through God's invention: forgiveness. The hurts received are unmerited, but recognize that in this world people are unfair to each other and can hurt one another deeply.

Remember, God forgave first. He wants to lead you into wholeness by inviting you to forgive your mother. As your healing—through forgiveness—begins, know that the process towards wholeness for yourself and the restoration of your relationship with your mother can be lengthy.

1. Read 1 Corinthians 2:9 and consider this statement in light of your relationship with your mother.

a. Imagine, with your limited sight, what the best relationship is that you and your mother could have. Then write down what you would like God to have prepared for you concerning your relationship with your mother.

b. What is the condition for receiving the wonderful possibilities God has prepared?

c. Think about this condition. In view of your relationship with your mother, what does it mean to love the Lord?

2. Now we need to begin to look at the basics in the forgiveness process. Write out Proverbs 20:9.

We know the answer to the question in this verse: only our Lord Jesus is without sin and has a pure heart. Thus, you can realize that the hurts you received came from an imperfect mother who needs the Lord's grace through forgiveness just as you do. But this mental acknowledgment cannot be the answer to a healed heart. An encounter with your past needs to happen.

Early in this chapter, we mentioned that what hurt you in your past may be only a blurred picture now. In the second "Reflections" section, you were asked to begin writing down this picture. Read what you wrote. Then ask God to reveal any other areas of conflict and pain.

Since this recall process may be both mentally and emotionally difficult, take time now or in the near future to write a letter to God to let Him know how you feel about your past. Express these emotions, and in doing so release them into His hands so He can make your heart new.

Recognize that in writing a letter to God, you are saying to Him that you want life, not death, with your mother. By committing your past on paper, you are facing the hurts, however minute or major. And by addressing this letter to our Lord, you are releasing your pain to Him.

3. a. Read John 10:10 and 1 John 3:14. How do these verses relate to the process of forgiving your mother?

    b. What do you believe will happen to this relationship if you fail to love your mother through forgiving her?

    c. Who is the one that wants to destroy this relationship?

4. Read and write down Ephesians 4:31-32.

If there is still some anger that you are harboring toward your mom, take time now to confess that to the Lord. Then ask

God to enable you to forgive your mother. (You may want to be specific about the areas you wrote in your letter.)

Another factor you need to recognize as you begin to forgive your mother is that she may not be able to enter into this process with you, and your relationship may not be restored. But forgiveness on your part will ultimately lead to your wholeness—a new heart—so that your past will not hinder the way you nurture your own child in his or her early developmental stages.

5. Read Psalm 147:3. What is God promising to do for you as a result of the forgiveness process?

6. God wants to give you other things through the healing He does.

> a. Read Ezekiel 36:24-27 and write down the gifts He wants to give you today, just as He gave them to His people, the house of Israel.

> b. With this new heart, ask God to show you your mother's strengths and attributes. Write them down and consider how you can encourage her to utilize them in her role as a grandmother.

CONCLUDING THOUGHTS

As you release to the Lord the feelings you have held onto from your past, He will give you a new heart, a new spirit to love your mother. No matter how she feels toward you, God will enable you to love her and see her as a human being created in His image.

Hopefully, you will begin to see the renewal taking place in your relationship with your mother, and will start to form a new kinship with her. You will begin to appreciate her as a person in ways you never could. You will see her strengths and acknowledge them to her.

You can love her in spite of her personal weaknesses. And you will see her as Jesus does—an individual with needs, desires, hurts, and confusions. You will be Jesus to her and share His grace. Ask Him to give you courage to take the next step toward wholeness—extending His love to her.

As a new mother, and now a "new" daughter, ponder what Sheila Kitzinger challenges you to implement as you help your mother define her role as a grandmother:

> We need to find a more positive role for grandmothers in our society, and to discover a new dignity and potential for creative achievement in the woman who has brought up her family who, because of all she has learned from this experience, may have a great deal to contribute to society.[8]

PRAYERS AND ANSWERS

What is the specific prayer you have at this point concerning your relationship with your mother?

Pray for discernment and wisdom to recognize the yoke God

wants you to wear as a mother as opposed to the one society dangles in front of you, tempting you to grab.

Pray for the mothers you know personally who have unreconciled relationships with their mothers.

Pray about any anxiety or insecurity you still sense lingering within you as a new mother.

Thank our Lord for the heart changes that have begun to take place during this fourth month.

Offer a prayer of thanksgiving to the Father for your mother.

"The family roles of women provide a meeting ground for the interweaving of generations. The caring orientation of adult daughters and their mothers—the centrality of mothering in both of their lives—means that their lives are linked from generation to generation."

Lucy Rose Fischer
Linked Lives

NOTES:
1. Sheila Kitzinger, *Women as Mothers* (New York: Random House, 1978), page 161.
2. Selma Fraiberg, *Every Child's Birthright* (New York: Basic Books, 1977), page 28.
3. Fraiberg, *Every Child's Birthright.*
4. As quoted by Anita Shreve in *Remaking Motherhood* (New York: Viking Penguin, Inc., 1987), page 125.
5. Wanda Urbanska, *The Singular Generation* (Garden City, N.Y.: Doubleday, 1986), page 163.
6. Shreve, *Remaking Motherhood*, pages 124-125.
7. John and Paula Sandford, *The Transformation of the Inner Man* (Tulsa, Okla.: Victory House, Inc., 1982), pages 148, 150.
8. Kitzinger, *Women as Mothers*, page 189.

CONTEMPLATING THE CALL

Envision a jigsaw puzzle laid out on a table. Many of the interlocking pieces are already joined together and you can see that the picture forming is of you—as a mother.

In the previous four months you have learned many skills and accomplished hours of hard work. In addition, you have been interpreting and creating an image of yourself as a mother. These past months represent the pieces of the puzzle you have already skillfully assembled. But the picture is incomplete. The puzzle requires still more creative thought.

As the physical adjustments of the early months become less prominent, what are you thinking about regarding your five months of motherhood experience? If you have not already done so, I challenge you to think about some of the issues that shape the image of motherhood and reflect on how you as a Christian are responding to these issues. These thoughts represent the next pieces you will fit into your puzzle.

You have become a mother at a time in history when the

meaning of that role is undergoing constant scrutiny. Not only are you working out your personal journey of mothering, but you are doing so in a culture that is highly focused on questions about mothering. Our culture's answers to the puzzle of mothering form a very odd, and often confusing, picture. The picture shows the great extremes to which people have gone in making an image of mothering that appeals to their needs.

In a span of ten months, two articles—both cover stories—were published that vividly illustrate two extremely different trends that presently shape our culture's puzzle of motherhood.

The first article was written for *Newsweek*. Titled "Three's a Crowd," the article observes that "faced with new options, many wives decide that motherhood is not an essential or even desirable role."[1]

The couples interviewed had chosen not to have children and gave reasons for their decision: lifestyle, work, money, freedom, relationship, personality, social views, and attitude. Birth control, voluntary sterilization, and abortion make such a choice possible. These couples saw children as a roadblock to their personal plans, and frankly expressed their disinclination to become mothers and fathers.

Then, in June of 1987, *Life* published "Baby Craving: Facing Widespread Infertility a Generation Presses the Limits of Medicine and Morality." This article portrayed three couples who are intensely seeking to be parents. The journalist writes, "Yes, say many men and women now eager to share their love with a baby after years in which their world revolved around themselves."[2]

The couples in this second article are saying "yes" to the many means now offered for enhancing fertility: acupuncture, psychic guidance, adoption, open adoption, and surrogacy. The desire for a child drives them to incredible lengths of endurance and financial expenditure. These women seek motherhood desperately.

Of course, these two groups represent the extremes in our culture—women who desire no children, and infertile women (or couples) who are trying everything possible to have a child. Most women in the United States probably fit into the puzzle somewhere between these extremes.

I do not propose to critique our cultural condition here, but I do wish to present the variety of issues that currently shape our society, so we can see the incredible atmosphere in which we are endeavoring to discover our identity as mothers. Look at some of the pieces of the puzzle:

- Abortions—a mother in our country has the legal right to terminate a pregnancy.
- Surrogate mothers—for a fee, a woman will bear a child for another, after receiving the man's sperm.
- Sperm bank mothers—a woman can become a mother by buying sperm donated to a sperm bank. No husband figure is necessary in her life, nor is a father figure provided for her child.
- Never mothers—an increasing number of married women are choosing not to be mothers because it would interrupt their careers or other priorities for fulfillment.
- Birth control—the use of contraceptives gives a woman more control in family planning.
- Single mothers—many women today are raising children by themselves, whether widowed, separated, divorced, or unmarried by choice.
- Teenage pregnancies—ever-increasing numbers of teenagers are becoming pregnant.
- Gay parenting—homosexuals are obtaining children in order to experience family.

You could add more examples to this list of mothering configurations, simply by searching the daily media. But overall, these are the issues and images of motherhood that bombard our minds. As Christian women, we are affected by our culture. But to what extent? Where do we fit into society's puzzle of motherhood, if at all? I encourage you in your fifth month to consider our culture's impact on your life as your piece together your motherhood puzzle.

──────────────────── REFLECTIONS ────────────────────

Why, in your opinion, do such radical departures from the traditional nuclear family exist today?

What is your inner response to these changes?

Do you feel secure with yourself as a mother, or is it difficult for you to explain why you are a mother (other than the basic biological fact of your being one)?

Is motherhood something one can choose to mold into any shape one wishes?

What further reflections regarding your body and mind can you make about your fifth month as a mother?

───────────────┤ HEART AND SPIRIT ├───────────────

The above discussion about our present culture as it relates to motherhood leads us to the deeper need to explore the spiritual dimensions of motherhood. A vital question is whether or not motherhood is a spiritual calling from God, and if so, what does that calling mean?

As Christians, we need to be developing a biblical theology that adequately undergirds our present role as mothers. Answers from twenty or thirty years ago may not be sufficient to handle the confusing pressures and technological realities that surround us. What scriptural knowledge will help us form our identity as mothers in the midst of great societal flux?

As a place to begin, consider Proverbs 29:18 (NASB), "Where there is no vision, the people are unrestrained." This wise saying is easy to ascribe to mothers. Without a vision of who we are and what purpose we have in the great scheme of things, we may wander unrestrained from one image of motherhood to another, never fully grasping our true value in God's creation of families and the world community. If we have no vision, we may lose all motivation to be mothers.

So what vision will keep us alive and growing? As is typical with Scripture, once we begin our search for answers, we discover multiple layers of knowledge. Therefore, we do not claim to have unearthed an entire biblical theology of motherhood—just a beginning. Your challenge is to continue to correct and build on what we have begun.

1. Read Genesis 1:27-28. What is apparently the first command God gave to Adam and Eve after their creation?

God gave Eve life, placed her in relationship with Adam, and then called her into motherhood. The name *Eve* means "life." In a very real sense, we would not be here today without her acceptance of God's plan for her to be a mother.

2. Eve had her first child after the Fall. Read Genesis 4:1. Who does Eve credit for the creation and safe delivery of the child?

3. With the birth of this first child after the Fall, what plan had God begun to unfold for humanity? (See Matthew 1:1-16.)

Thus, from the account of Eve, Scripture's very first mother, we learn that:

- God desired for Adam and Eve to have children.
- God creates children and enables women to deliver them.
- God has a loving purpose in the creation of children that extends throughout salvation history.

4. After Eve, many other mothers enter biblical history. Read about Sarah in Genesis 17:16. Again, Scripture shows that God is Lord of the womb and that He directs when life will begin there. What is the promise God makes concerning Sarah:

For her near future?

For far into the future?

5. Read about Hannah in 1 Samuel 1:26-28.

a. In your own words, what does she say to the priest Eli about her firstborn son?

b. What role does prayer play in her first experience of motherhood?

c. What is her response to God regarding the child's life?

6. Then, there is Mary, the mother of Jesus. Read what she says to the angel after being told that she has been chosen to be the mother of the Savior (Luke 1:38). Describe Mary's attitude with at least three adjectives:

From the stories of these three mothers, we can build our understanding of God and motherhood through several observations:

- God continually creates children and chooses specific women to be their mothers.
- In each case, there is evidence of a relationship between God and the mother that precedes the birth of the child and affirms the mother as she begins her experience of motherhood. "Blessed is she who has believed that what the Lord has said to her will be accomplished!" (Luke 1:45).
- In each instance, a great purpose in the history of God's people is served through the woman's willingness to accept God's call through bearing the child.

CONCLUDING THOUGHTS

How does the study of these biblical women relate to us? Are we still called to be mothers? What does this calling mean in a century of birth control, career opportunities, and nuclear bombs?

Sidney Callahan explores these issues in her book *The Illusion of Eve: Modern Woman's Quest for Identity*. She describes in general terms the two current philosophical extremes about women and motherhood. First, there are those who propose that women are entirely shaped by their culture. This philosophy states that society programs females from birth to be mothers and that if this were not so, women might not choose or even desire to be mothers. The other extreme argues that women are biologically designed to be mothers. Therefore, nature is the most important determinant of her personhood.[3]

If left to choose one or the other of these philosophical paths to motherhood, I would indeed feel hopeless. To believe that my culture has entirely determined who I am would make me feel depersonalized and vulnerable to any change that comes along. On the other hand, to say that I have no role other than motherhood because I was born with female reproductive organs is equally disheartening. Is there another choice for me as a woman? Yes, there is.

The God of Sarah, Hannah, and Mary has revealed Himself in Jesus Christ. We can choose to follow Jesus Christ and be free of cultural and natural determinism. He is established as Lord of all, and He glorifies neither culture nor nature. Christ reveals that God is the One who best leads us in life. Regarding Mark 3:34-35, Callahan writes, "Sexual identity, family relationships—all are transcended by 'whoever does the will of God.' Women therefore are also called."[4] Clearly, we are called to follow Christ, but what does a call to motherhood mean?

God is revealed in Scripture as One who makes a covenant with His people; His covenant is to love them with a steadfast love as they seek to know and obey Him. To be called by God is to realize that He alone can sustain your relationship with Himself. God is in covenant partnership with you as the mother of the child He has given to you. This task of loving would be impossible if it were not for God's promise to help you at all times. The mother's call to be committed to her child is not a demand for perfection. God's covenant works in such a way that "the first sign of a contradiction in committed relationships is not the end but the beginning of covenant love. . . . Where dead ends and repeated failures occur, a new pilgrimage can take place."[5] This fact of God's covenant love is a great encouragement to those who follow Christ and is especially relevant to mothers.

God has created marriage as a covenant for two people to love one another as He has loved. In your case, He has created a child for you and your husband to love with the same covenant love He shows to all His children. As you consider your calling, try to spend time in Scripture. Study the passages that deal with God's covenant love (Exodus 34:10, Leviticus 26:12, Isaiah 55:3, Mark 14:24, Ephesians 5:1-2).

The call to be a mother is part of the all-encompassing call to be a Christian. Your female biology is important and dignified because God created you and will resurrect you. But your body, your entire self, is primarily to be brought before God through prayer in order to receive His guidance.

So, yes, if God has placed a life in your arms, you have received a direct call from Him to extend His covenant love to that child. You are involved in a deeply spiritual adventure. You have all the vast resources of God's love, forgiveness, and renewal at your disposal as you fulfill your call to be a mother.

Through your knowledge of God and the Scriptures, you have a vision for children, community, world, and history that cannot be rivaled by any world philosophy. Pray that the Holy Spirit will give you, and all of us as mothers, God's vision of who we are to be and how we are to walk in that vision every day.

PRAYERS AND ANSWERS

What are some of the answers to last month's prayers?

What prayers are you still waiting to have answered, and how do you feel about waiting?

What is on your heart this month for prayer?

Pray for mothers of our generation who are searching for guidance—that their search would lead them to Christ.

Pray for mothers who are in poverty situations.

"But Pam, do think! Don't you see you are not beginning at all as long as you are in that state of mind? You're treating God only as a means to Michael. But the whole thickening treatment consists in learning to want God for His own sake."
    "You wouldn't talk like that if you were a mother."

"You mean, if I were only a mother. But there is no such thing as being only a mother. You exist as Michael's mother only because you first exist as God's creature. That relation is older and closer."

C.S. Lewis
The Great Divorce

NOTES:
1. "Three's a Crowd," *Newsweek*, September 1, 1986, page 69.
2. "Baby Craving: Facing Widespread Infertility a Generation Presses the Limits of Medicine and Morality," *Life*, June 1987, page 26.
3. Sidney Callahan, *The Illusion of Eve: Modern Woman's Quest for Identity* (New York: Sheed and Ward, 1965), pages 13-33.
4. Callahan, *The Illusion of Eve*, page 37.
5. Ray Anderson and Dennis Guernsey, *On Being Family: a Social Theology of the Family* (Grand Rapids: Eerdmans Publishing Co., 1985), page 45.

SITTING AT HIS FEET

BODY AND MIND

Since my childhood days, I have had many opportunities to hike in the mountains. Tromping through the leaves, over tree roots, and up the steep paths and jagged rocks is exhilarating. Now that I am older, a day in the mountains renews me—soul and body.

Reaching the top of a mountain, after much physical exertion, is well worth the strain. I can see for miles in all directions. At the top, I am halfway through my day's journey and have time to rest and reflect. So please sit with me for awhile on the mountaintop. You, too, have completed half of your journey.

Six months of mothering are now or soon will be behind you. Pause to reflect on the miles you've hiked thus far and to refuel for the months ahead. Look with me at the valleys and hills below to view what you will encounter.

Many changes will now occur quickly with your child, leading to more independence for both of you. This month your child is both physically and emotionally ready to begin weaning, a process he or she will more than likely help initiate. (Weaning does not happen immediately, but probably will be completed by your child's first birthday.) Your child is eating more solid foods, and increasing his or her mobility. New areas of exploration are open to your child as he or she begins to crawl and sit up and the interest in nursing begins to wane.

If you have nursed your child, physical changes will occur in you during weaning. Your hormones will revert to their normal state prior to pregnancy. This transition can cause you to be on an emotional rollercoaster, for lactation usually takes three to four months to stop completely. The size of your breasts will change—again. They will not return to their normal size for several months. Also, unless you gradually wean your child, omitting one feeding at a time, the weaning process could be physically painful.

Other changes are occurring, whether or not you are nursing. Since your child is moving away from you to investigate his or her world, your constant mental attention is no longer needed. Hence, you receive some "breathing space." This space will give you time to consider carefully the personal choices you have to make—ones that will affect you and your family now and in the years ahead.

Making Important Choices
Throughout this study, we have talked about the influence our culture has had on motherhood. Last month you contemplated whether or not God has called you to be a mother, in a society that cannot even agree on what motherhood is or is not. This month we want to focus on the mothering choices you personally have to make: whether or not to combine a career with mothering; whether to return to work outside the home or combine a home business with mothering; or whether or not to be an "at-home" mother. Each

choice has its own challenges and responsibilities, which we will discuss.

While resting on the mountain, sit at the feet of Jesus and ask Him to speak to you about your choice. Allow Him to see into your heart and examine your motives and intentions. Let Him give you peace and certainty that the decision you make is His good and perfect will for you and your family.

When making any major decision, you have to consider the factors that influence your choice. Five main areas may determine your personal choice: society, personal family background, your identity, your family's needs, and your Christian faith. Let's briefly examine each one of them.

As we scrutinize society's current view of mothering, we see contradictions. On the one hand, we see a generation that for the first time sees parenting as optional. A recent newspaper headline declared: "'Baby bust' threatens to change American society." The article said that the declining domestic birthrates are "so low they are not producing enough children to replace their populations."[1] On the other hand, women are having second thoughts about sacrificing all for a career. Those without children realize that the "biological clock" does not reverse. They ask, "Should I change my professional goals, since my work won't last forever, and have a child instead?"

Also, women who have children are stretching maternity leaves longer and even dropping out of the managerial work force to take part-time work or establish home businesses. They want more time with their children. No matter which option you choose, society has failed "to make motherhood an attractive 'choice,'" a respected profession.[2]

Anita Shreve, author of *Remaking Motherhood*, speaks emphatically about society's lack of concern or dignity for motherhood:

It is not respected in the workplace, as working mothers discover when they need time off to care for young children; it is not respected in society at large, as working mothers discover when they try to find adequate childcare for their infants; and it is not respected among peers, as at-home mothers discover when they are called upon to account for themselves in social groups. To 'just be a mother' in this decade, in this country, is perceived as having failed in some fundamental way.[3]

Another area that influences your decision is your personal background. We discussed in Chapter Four how your mother's values and beliefs contributed to your definition of a good mother. Now you may find yourself struggling against this "perfect mother" image. You may find yourself disagreeing with her values.

Remember that society tried to tell our mothers that to be a good mother, all one's energies must be focused on the child. But now that you're a mother, you see motherhood as only one of several life roles. You see the need to continue growing in other areas of life, whether that be outside or within the home.

Your family is another major determinant in your choice. You need to seriously examine your "family's goals, finances, priorities and values; your own needs, professional as well as maternal; and your baby's emotional and physical needs."[4]

Your source of self-worth and identity also influences your choice. When you seek your identity in positions, they become idols. Then you forget your first love, the Lord Jesus. Only disappointment and unhappiness will follow if you look to external roles for your self-worth.

Many women feel stretched between two extremes—

having a career or staying at home. They may ask themselves, *Do only two choices exist?* Neither seems quite right to them. But the Lord Jesus frees you from having to adopt one "right way" or from being controlled by society's proclamation that only two choices are available. He is the Liberator who affirms you in your womanhood as you seek Him for the right choice during this season in your life.

As you consider each choice, critically ask yourself, *What is determining my decision?* Only our Lord can help you decide the path you should choose. Ask Him to eliminate any factor that would hinder you from making the right choice.

Facing the Challenges of Your Choice

Now that we have looked at the factors that influence your choice, let's examine the challenges each choice may bring.

When combining a career and motherhood, you will juggle many challenges. First, you and many other women who have chosen this route are pioneers. You have no previous generation's knowledge or advice to draw on to make your dual roles work. And often, your choice to have a career threatens society and the church.

So where does this leave you? As a Christian, you and your husband first need to agree that returning to your career is right for the entire family. With this agreement, you should be at peace that your career is where God wants you, which will give you strength to handle the challenges you will encounter as a working mother.

One of the sacrifices you have to make as a working mother is placing your child under surrogate care and giving up the quantity time you have with him or her. You may find yourself caught in the conflict of quality time versus quantity time. I caution you against letting quality time "be transformed into a rigid code, with specific do's and don'ts," where you begin to believe that the time you spend with your child "after work must be consistently superior and free from strife."[5]

As one mother said, and more than likely she's speaking for many mothers, "When I came home from work at six-thirty at night I just tried to cram everything in. I tried to be super perfect. Everything he wasn't getting all day had to happen in the hour and a half before he went to bed."[6]

Another challenge is finding the right surrogate care for your child. Without sounding pious or trying to zip through a crucial and major issue for you, I truly encourage you to pray earnestly about this matter. Inquire at your church about child care or ask other working mothers for suggestions. Also, seek your husband's help and support. Both you and your husband need to decide who will take care of your child.

To make life easier, seek others to help with tasks that take away the limited nurturing time you have with your child. If financially possible, buy services such as house cleaning, lawn care, meal preparation, and clothing repair. And the next time you go shopping, peruse the magazine stand for other suggestions and encouragement from working mothers. Several publications are available for career mothers. One is specifically titled *Working Mother*.

If you are a mother who is reluctantly returning to work because of financial necessity, you must work through the same challenges as a mother who has the choice to return to her career. You will also encounter at least one challenge unique to your situation. This challenge is the stress that may occur between you and your husband due to differing opinions of whether your working is a financial necessity. To help alleviate this tension, strive for open and honest communication with your husband.

You and your husband could both compile a list of the

"positives" and the "negatives" of your returning to work or staying at home. Then sit down together and compare your lists. Work together to achieve a realistic compromise of what is best for your family now and in the future. Reach an agreement on a suitable income for your family's particular needs. With this agreement, you will both know if you need to work full time or part time, and when you should return to work.

During this decision-making time, seek out another mother you trust. She can listen to you with love and empathy and possibly give you the positive perspective you need in order to see your situation clearly.

If you choose to combine motherhood with a home-based business, you have challenges as well. Your choice of work allows you some flexibility with your schedule as opposed to a strict 9 to 5 routine. You can, for example, work during your child's nap times. But when your child begins to take only one nap, you, too, will need to decide about child care.

Like the mother who works outside the home, you may want to buy services to take care of your household chores. The more tasks you eliminate from your daily agenda, the more "quality time" you have with your child.

One excellent resource for home-business mothers is an organization called "Mother's Home Business Network." With a membership, you receive a year's subscription (four issues) to their publication, *Homeworking Mothers*, and a free classified ad in the publication to communicate your business to other mothers. You also receive a copy of their booklet, *Mothers' Money Making Manual*, and the annual directory of members, *Mothers' Mailpak*. Their address is: Mother's Home Business Network, P.O. Box 423, East Meadow, NY 11554.

Deciding to be an at-home mother is no easy choice, just

as returning to work is no easy choice. The only differences between the at-home mother and the career-seeking mother are the challenges each faces.

A Sunday edition of the cartoon "The Family Circus," captured perfectly how many people view a mother who stays at home. The first panel shows the mother in her front doorway holding her youngest son, who is in diapers and is clutching a dripping spoon. She is talking with a woman, dressed in a business suit and holding a clipboard, who is conducting a survey. The conversation proceeds as follows:

> The mother: "Why, no—I don't have employment outside the home."
> The woman: "I see—well . . . as a NON-WORKING MOTHER, what's your opinion on . . . ."

The woman's remark astounds the mother. In the second panel you see the mother—a blank stare on her face—imagining all the jobs she performs during a day: cooking, feeding, driving, dressing, cleaning. In the next panel the woman gets only one response to her question: the door is slammed in her face.

As a mother who has chosen to stay at home, you probably have encountered a scenario similar to the one described above. You are misunderstood. You are a novelty in today's society. "You're only a mother?" many may exclaim with astonishment.

The women's movement has offered the working mother answers to difficult questions about her life such as, "Why am I working? What can I expect there? Where will it take me?"[7] But it has not assisted the at-home mother with answers to the questions that concern her: "Why stay at home? How can I find satisfaction there? How does life at home fit with important things in my family's life or the fabric of the larger community?"[8]

Besides being misunderstood and feeling that others are indifferent toward your questions, an at-home mother faces another major challenge—contentment. You need to be content in your workplace—the home—and in your heart and mind that you made the right choice. You need not feel ashamed because you are not employed. Nor should you think you are "engaged in a second-rate occupation which no intelligent, up-to-date woman could possibly endure for more than a few hours."[9]

Like Deborah Fallows said in her book, *A Mother's Work*, "I was not choosing to stay home because I liked housework, but because I wanted to take more responsibility for raising my children."[10]

An advantage you, as an at-home mother, have is your unstructured time. This may be a challenge for you. The only schedule you really have to follow is your child's. Other than that you determine each day's timetable. Since your child is probably on a predictable schedule, a carefully structured day may help you gain confidence in your role. Accomplishing specific tasks may improve the way you see yourself, especially if you have left a career to be at home.

Now that your time is at least somewhat your own, you have seemingly endless possibilities to utilize your talents. Don't let your home be a place of drudgery. Instead, make it a place of creativity. Take time not only to keep your talents and skills refined, but keep your mind stimulated and challenged by reading and becoming aware of current events. Your spiritual life can grow too, if you use your free time for prayer and study.

An excellent source of encouragement for you could be the nonprofit organization, "Mothers At Home." They are devoted to supporting mothers who choose to stay home and nurture their families. One of their goals is to place mothers across the country in touch with each other through their monthly publication, *Welcome Home*. They also desire to correct society's misconception and the media's misrepresentation of mothering—for both the mother at home and the employed mother.

You can obtain more information about their organization and subscribe to their magazine by writing: Mothers At Home, P.O. Box 2208, Merrifield, VA 22116.

To this point we have examined the challenges unique to each individual choice of mothering. One challenge faces all mothers, no matter which course they take. This challenge is the ambivalence and guilt you may feel about the decisions you have made. Inevitably the questions surface: "Am I making the right choice by working?" "By staying at home?" "By working in my home?"

The guilt may come from a myriad of sources: the "who" or "what" that influenced your decision. If you have chosen to work, guilt may come from the voices in your past that say, "Mothers don't work," "My mother didn't work," "I'm neglecting my child." If you are at home, your guilt may come from the voices of society or your peers, causing you to feel isolated—like you belong in the Dark Ages.

Whatever your particular source of guilt, you need to pinpoint the specific reasons for it. If you have truly sought the Lord's will prior to your decision, you can say with assurance that you're where you should be. Begin praying for the Lord to bring a nondefensive stance to your decision.

Bearing Responsibility for Your Choice

No major choice can be made without responsibilities. Four responsibilities are attached to your choice.

First, you need to know why you made your particular choice and be at peace with your decision. Your child needs to see you content, enjoying your chosen work.

Second, you need to know that your choice was the Lord's desire for your family. One mother speaks, gratefully, about the God who meets us in our unique situations:

> Until recently, we often felt we were blazing new trails alone, yet we strongly felt this was how God was directing us. . . . I realize the way God has directed us is not a blanket outline for all families, but we are continually reminded through Scripture study that one of the awesome aspects of God's nature is his ability to treat each individual as unique.[11]

Therefore, "the Christian responsibility . . . is to evaluate how well the individuals within the family are doing and determine one's own actions for the common good of all."[12]

Third, you need to allow the Holy Spirit to free you from guilt. He alone can work in you a spirit of harmony and certainty.

Fourth, you need to realize, as a mother, that your nurturing years are only for a season. God has given you talents and abilities. He wants you to be a responsible citizen of His Kingdom and use them for His redeeming purpose and goodwill. Heed the words of Dorothy R. Pape, author of *In Search of God's Ideal Woman:*

> It is wonderful to be a mother in the Lord's will and with his guidance. . . . I think I could not have been as much help to the children if I had not already had some wider interests than my own housekeeping. And if my whole purpose in life were just to bring them successfully to maturity, what a bleak prospect would await me now, with both of them in another country and my husband away so much. It is when we are really seeking first the kingdom of God and his righteousness

that he adds the other blessings. We must not be possessive and value our children more than the Lord himself.[13]

You cannot let His gifts to you lie dormant and unused until you are no longer "mothering." Seek Him now, and ask Him how He wants you to utilize your gifts, even if it's only a small portion at this time in your life. Be a wise steward of all He has entrusted to you.

───────────────── REFLECTIONS ─────────────────

What criteria do you think a mother should consider in deciding to work or stay at home?

List the highest values/priorities that must be weighed in each situation. Give the pros and cons for each choice.

Which factors are most important to you?

Ask yourself if society's rules and standards are influencing your choice. If so, where?

In view of the culture's contradictions, in what ways does your faith in the Lord Jesus influence your decision?

What specific challenges do you think you will encounter with your choice?

Have you experienced ambivalence or guilt regarding your decision? If so, what is the source of these feelings?

In which areas do you need more support from your family, relatives, friends, workplace, and church?

┤ HEART AND SPIRIT ├

"Know also that wisdom is sweet to your soul; if you find it, there is a future hope for you, and your hope will not be cut off."

Proverbs 24:14

On the bookcase sat the box. A silk floral design covered its exterior. In between each flower pattern was a circular motif, the Chinese symbol for prosperity. The interior, lined with white silk, held fine stationery. Until recently, it had only been a reminder of my first Christmas with Daniel.

One afternoon, I stared at this box. (Asher was now a part of our family and had been for almost six months.) Tears rolled down my cheeks. God was speaking to me.

I saw all of who I was and had been, prior to becoming a mother, inside the box. Inside, I was an abyss. Outside, I was a mother, dressed in a role that did not fit.

I realized how much I wanted to throw away my "new clothes" and take on those of my past. I wanted my talents and gifts back. I didn't want them to stay inside the box, never to be used again.

The void within me seemed to grow darker and deeper. What had once brought me joy and fulfillment now sat silent inside the box. My gifts, like the fine stationery, appeared worthless as they laid dormant and hidden away.

At that point, I knew the box no longer belonged to me. I could not possess my talents and abilities. I stretched out my hands and gave it back to the Lord.

As I released the box to Jesus, I knew He was now

responsible for my life and the direction it would take from now on, with or without the fine treasures inside the box. I knew He would make the appropriate alterations so that my new role would fit me.

Before I stood up, my eyes were drawn to the Chinese motif on the box. Faith and hope replaced the empty pit inside of me. God was my prosperity in life. I knew that I was His workmanship, created in Christ Jesus to do good works, which God prepared in advance for me to do. He would fulfill His purpose for me.

Since that day, when my box became a personal proverb from the Spirit of God, I have gathered more wisdom and understanding about what God desires of us as mothers. Let's examine what life and freedom we have in our Lord Jesus.

In Ecclesiastes 3:1, we are told that "there is a time for everything, and a season for every activity under heaven." Thus, if we are honest with ourselves, we must realize "motherhood isn't forever . . . . Once we are mothers, of course, we remain mothers for the rest of our lives, but the intensity with which we apply ourselves to that role is limited to a predictable few years between the birth and maturation of our child."[14]

You need to begin preparing now for the next season in your life. You do not want to awaken one morning, middle-aged, your children grown, your husband completely absorbed in his work, with your talents and "skills scattered like decade-old tulip bulbs that still" sprout "green leaves but . . . no longer produce flowers."[15] You need to ask the Lord today to show you where He wants you to channel your talents and energies and what course you need to chart for the future.

1. In preparation, even at this young stage in your mothering experience, read Luke 10:38-42 and write out verses 41 and 42.

2. Do you see yourself as a Martha or a Mary in these verses? Why?

3. Have you been putting your roles and responsibilities in life ahead of your identity as a disciple of Jesus?

4. Why does Jesus want you to be like Mary?

When you sit at the feet of Jesus, you will know what choices to make during this season of mothering and what choices to make for the future regarding your talents. Only by listening to Him can you prepare for the days ahead.

5.   a. Read Romans 12:1-2. Write in your own words what the Lord wants you to set at His feet.

   b. How do you see this offering in relation to the choices you need to make . . .

Now?

In the future?

6. Where do you need the Lord to change your mind . . .

About your identity as a mother?

In the choices you are facing?

The Lord promises that, with your mind transformed, you will be able to know "his good, pleasing and perfect will."

7. a. In what areas are you still uncertain about His will concerning the choices you need to make?

    b. In what areas are you struggling with where your energies need to be directed at this time?

8. What, in your "box," do you need to give to the Lord?

The maturing process, through sacrifice, allows you to become a good steward of all the Lord has given you—your child, your talents, and your abilities. You will be able to acknowledge that you receive your identity in Him, not through any role—even that of a mother. You will be able to use your gifts as a responsible ambassador for Jesus, not for selfish gain or your self-worth.

Even during this season of mothering, our Lord does not want to limit you but to help you choose the right paths—the paths that are best for you, your husband, and your child now and in the future.

9.   a. Read and write down Colossians 2:6-8,10.

      b. Why do you need to be strengthened in your faith, especially at this time in your life?

10. Have you been deceived and taken captive in any way . . .

Concerning what a mother does or doesn't do?

In the choice you have made or are considering?

11. Has your choice been made through the principles of this world or through our Lord's?

Before we go our separate ways this month, thank you for sitting with me on the mountain and listening to my heart and searching for His wisdom in your particular situation.

Allow the Lord to give you your identity, not your roles. Allow Him to show you which choice to make. Allow Him to prepare you for the other seasons in your life. Your gifts and talents will then serve Him, and you can introduce other mothers, who seek to have genuine worth and dignity, to the Prince of Peace and the True Liberator: Jesus Christ.

--------------------| PRAYERS AND ANSWERS |--------------------

Pray for wisdom and peace concerning the choice you must make.

Pray specifically for strength and courage to meet the challenges your choice brings.

Ask God to renew your mind so that you are certain your identity is in Him.

Ask God to show you how to be a good steward of your talents and gifts during these early days of mothering, and how you should prepare for the next season in your life.

Pray that your church will encourage and support mothers.

Pray for unity and harmony among mothers who have careers and mothers who are at home.

Ask the Lord to show you how you can have a godly influence on mothers who are struggling with their personal identity.

Give thanks to the Lord for His goodness and care of you and your child through the last six months.

"Instead of blindly following custom or tradition, it seems best for women to 'choose that good part,' like Mary, and sit at Christ's feet to hear instructions for each situation as it arises; then . . . to follow them."

Dorothy R. Pape
In Search of God's Ideal Woman

"We women have a tremendous influence, not only upon our husbands and children, but upon society, as well. We have a responsibility beyond ourselves, whether our career takes us outside the home or not. The next generation depends upon the choices women make today."

Dee Jepsen
Women: Beyond Equal Rights

NOTES:
 1. *The Atlanta Journal and Constitution*, July 5, 1987, Section C, page 1C.
 2. Anita Shreve, *Remaking Motherhood* (New York: Viking Penguin, Inc., 1987), page 124.
 3. Shreve, *Remaking Motherhood*, pages 124-125.
 4. Barbara T. Berg, *The Crisis of the Working Mother* (New York: Simon & Schuster, 1986), page 60.
 5. Berg, *The Crisis of the Working Mother*, page 79.
 6. Berg, *The Crisis of the Working Mother*, page 77.
 7. Deborah Fallows, *A Mother's Work* (Boston: Houghton Mifflin Co., 1985), page 218.
 8. Fallows, *A Mother's Work*, page 218.
 9. Sheila Kitzinger, *Women as Mothers* (New York: Random House, 1978), page 32.
10. Fallows, *A Mother's Work*, page 27.
11. Linda Kunz, "Letters to the Editor," *InterVarsity*, Spring 1987, page 2.
12. Sidney Cornelia Callahan, *The Illusion of Eve: Modern Woman's Quest for Identity* (New York: Sheed and Ward, 1965), page 157.
13. Dorothy R. Pape, *In Search of God's Ideal Woman* (Downers Grove, Ill.: Inter-Varsity Press, 1977), pages 354-355.
14. Nancy Rubin, *The Mother Mirror* (New York: Putnam's Sons, 1984), page 263.
15. Rubin, *The Mother Mirror*, page 23.

BECOMING A SERVANT

BODY AND MIND

The last time you looked at the magazines in your supermarket, do you recall seeing one entitled *Servant*? Have you read any woman's magazine with articles explaining the "how tos" of serving others? Probably not—on both counts.

Self-centeredness is omnipresent in every generation and "self-denial is the perennial challenge of humanity."[1] As Christians, we exchange easy-to-fulfill self-centeredness for difficult-to-accomplish self-denial. In return, our Lord gives us a cross engraved with the word *servant*.

For the last seven months you have carried the cross of servanthood. Yet your cross came with an additional inscription, a specific calling to servanthood; your cross reads, "Mother." No doubt you have come to recognize that Jesus' call to servanthood is perhaps the most arduous task He has given us. Becoming a servant in the role of mother doesn't happen instantly, or without sacrifice. Together let's look at what you have encountered (or will encounter) as you accept your calling to be a servant in the role of mother.

103

The Sacrifices of Servanthood
Time is a precious commodity that you have had to sacrifice as you have assumed the role of mother. Time alone, or with your husband, is now minimal. No longer can you socialize with your friends or family as frequently as in the past. Even the spontaneity, which you and your husband both enjoyed prior to the birth of your child, is filed away under the letter "F," for future days.

With this loss of personal time you may experience feelings of isolation. You've had to sever commitments to the social and intellectual stimulation to which you were accustomed before. You may feel like your growth has been thwarted because the choices you now make must first focus on your baby's needs, not your own.

Part of being a servant involves a constant readiness to obey the master's requests. For you, this requires continual adjustment to your child's changing needs as he or she progresses through the stages of development. You may have thought your child would fit into your way of living, but this is not so. You have had to throw away your adult rules of time and put on your child's watch.

Even though you are on your child's timetable, you cannot exclude your own needs. So you are now in the process of learning, through trial and error, how to balance both your developmental needs and your child's.

Now that your child is no longer an immobile little bundle, you may be on call more than in the early months. Your child definitely wants more of your attention and may begin to move about the house this month. So you cannot just leave the child on the floor or in the playpen to entertain himself or herself.

Another dimension of serving your child means understanding your child's emotional development. This month you may see, for the first time, that your child's need for you goes beyond the physical. Your child now is beginning to realize he or she is a unique person, separate from you and your husband. Even though your child likes venturing away from you to explore, the new world he or she discovers is both exciting and frightening. Therefore, you must accept your child's increased need for your physical presence. Your child requires both independence and your continued involvement for emotional reassurance.[2]

You will also encounter your child's need to cling to recognized people. Not only does your child distinguish himself or herself as distinct from you, he or she also sees other people as different from you. When your child notices a new face, he or she scans the room for a familiar person to be near. Strangers have become people to fear.[3]

The initial bond of trust you and your child established in the first few weeks is now put to the test. Your child needs to know that you, and others he or she has become attached to, are available. At this point in your child's emotional growth, security and familiarity are essential.[4]

While you are adjusting to your child's changing emotional needs, you are probably still learning to accept the continuous, unpleasant, menial jobs that are required of a mother. At times you may feel that all your waking hours are spent changing diapers, feeding, dressing, bathing, and cleaning up after your baby.

For me, there were days when I just wanted to throw in the diaper, give up the servant business, pack my bags, and let someone else take over. After spending most of my day communicating with Asher, I sometimes felt like my brain was starting to shrivel. I was tired of being a servant! Yet at the end of those tedious, mundane days, I realized how blessed I was. Asher was becoming a little person—learning every day. He was no longer a helpless infant, and I saw that this stage of his life, which for me had been especially laborious and a true test of servanthood, was quickly coming to an end.

I was also blessed to have a healthy son, both physically and mentally. I haven't had to endure the pain of an ill child. You, however, may be a mother who serves a child with a chronic illness or handicap. You truly have learned sacrifice in a way most new mothers do not have to experience. Your baby's problems are an everyday affair. Physical and mental exhaustion are your constant companions.

I truly believe that when we call on God, He gives us the strength to handle each day's tasks of servanthood, even if our child is not well. Not only does He give us the needed strength, but He also asks us to mature in our attitude toward serving. He can transform the way we perceive our service.

During one of my grouchy, obstinate moments, when I was having trouble accepting my servant role, I read Jean Fleming's book *Between Walden and the Whirlwind*. While reading her chapter on service, I realized how God wanted me, as a mother, to view those disgusting, menial duties I had often abhorred. I knew He was asking me to grow up spiritually. I encourage you to consider the following thoughts from Jean Fleming, in light of your own circumstances:

> God's order is not to abolish the mundane and the routine from the life of a Christian, but to transform it.
> Because Christ lives in us all, our work can be spiritual work. He elevates all He touches, turning the distasteful job into a holy act of expression. Even in the ordinary duties of life, He will reveal Himself.[5]

Thus far we have discussed what you must sacrifice, learn, adjust to, and accept as a mother. We now need to discuss the anger and/or resentment that may arise due to your servant role.

The Struggles of Servanthood

Be encouraged! No one is instantly a willing and loving servant! You are not yet expected to be a perfect servant; you are in the process of "becoming." A major part of this "becoming" process occurs "precisely by enhancing the growth of others, in particular, those who have most need of us."[6]

One area in which you may harbor anger is in your lack of control over your daily routine. Because I am goal-oriented, relinquishing control has been difficult and frustrating for me. I have had to recognize—reluctantly at times—that I am in a waiting mode with Asher. I must serve him first and not myself.

In our angry, emotional moments, which result from our loss of control, we need to realize that "the goals and fulfillment of life as a parent remain very different from those . . . in the working world. They are less tangible: the needs of a growing child are not definable the way a job is. They are less predictable. . . . They are less immediate: parenting goes on from one day to the next, while a project at work can be wrapped up and completed."[7]

You may also struggle with meeting your child's relentless demands, another step in relinquishing control. Know that you are not alone in this tension. A recent published study, *The Motherhood Report*, surveyed mothers on various issues pertaining to mothering. The editors disclosed that "for most mothers, the dark side of infancy revolved around a feeling of bondage brought on by the relentless demands of caring for their babies. Many mothers spoke of the exhaustion and stress of being swallowed up by the total responsibility of caring for an infant."[8]

You may find yourself resenting your child for the interruptions he or she brings to your planned schedule. When you are on the telephone with a friend or conversing with your dinner guests, you may feel anger brewing within you because your child's needs prevent you from giving your undivided attention to your friends or guests.

A major step in working through the projected anger toward your child is to realize, in your mind and heart, that your child cannot meet his or her own needs. Your child depends on the willingness of someone else to provide the means of satisfaction and survival. You are your child's "someone else," the servant in the form of a mother.

"God has some service in mind for each of us"[9]—for you and me that is being a mother. "Our part is to give ourselves to Him, accepting the assignment He bestows."[10]

| REFLECTIONS |

In conjunction with mothering, define your role as a servant.

During the last seven months, which aspects of being a servant to your child have been most difficult?

What do you anticipate your personal struggle in becoming a servant will be in the months ahead?

How are you learning to balance your needs with your child's needs?

If you have an ill child, in which areas do you need specific encouragement and strength?

List specific ways you are projecting anger and resentment toward your child.

Reflect on the days that have passed since your child's birth. Evaluate how you have grown, both mentally and spiritually, since becoming a servant in a mother's role.

──────── HEART AND SPIRIT ────────

Who am I now? For you, the answer to this question has been shaped by several new roles over the last seven months.

In Chapter Four, the answer was that you are a mother, yet still a daughter. In Chapter Six, we looked at several possible choices for the answer: career with mothering; returning to work, yet reluctantly; a home business with mothering; or an "at-home" mother. This month we added another role—being a servant.

Over the past seven months you have discovered that motherhood brings "God-given distractions from self."[11] Through sacrifice, your character is being molded into the image of the perfect and complete servant, our Lord Jesus. To understand what is required of you as a servant, and to instill you with strength and courage to continue your "becoming" process, we need to study the Lord's example of servanthood.

1. Read Matthew 11:28-29 and write it out.

When we take on the role of a servant, we must know whose yoke we wear. We cannot serve two masters at once, or we will be encumbered with conflicting demands.

2. a. Since becoming a mother, have you tried to wear the yoke of the Lord and the yoke of self-centeredness?

b. If so, describe where you specifically need to be freed from the wrong yoke and where you need to receive rest. Tell the Lord about this.

Once you are freed, in all areas, from serving the wrong master, you must then follow the Lord's example of servanthood. In Paul's letter to Philippi, he tells us how we are to imitate Christ.

3. Read Philippians 2:1-11, focusing on verses 3-8. What are you instructed to do in verses 3-4?

4.   a. How have you been fulfilling these instructions during the last seven months?

b. How have you not?

5. As a mother, what should your attitude be (verses 5-8)?

6. We said earlier that Christ is the perfect and complete servant. In following His example, what within you must die on the cross so that you can become a more perfect servant?

7. Read John 13:1-17. Why do you think Jesus waited until His last supper with His disciples to give them His most important lesson and example of servanthood?

8. How is Jesus' last lesson relevant to your life?

9. In the context of your role as a mother, what do you think the Lord is specifically showing you to do through His example?

10. Do you realize that unless you allow the Lord to serve you, through a spiritual washing, you cannot have the strength or humility to serve others? Ask yourself how Jesus can serve you as a mother. What is His "foot washing" for you?

11. a. Why might you resist the Lord serving you, like Peter did when the Lord wanted to wash his feet?

    b. In what ways are you resisting what God wants to do in your life? Be specific.

12. Read 1 Peter 4:10-11. In wearing our Lord's yoke, we are required to use our gifts to serve others.

    a. What specific gifts has God given to you that enable you to be a good and faithful servant to your child?

b. How do you see these gifts as administering God's grace to your child?

13. a. God requires you to serve with the strength He has provided. Why?

b. In what ways have you been serving in your own strength?

In closing, I want to encourage you as you continue becoming a servant. I know the excruciating process involved in dying to the self-centered nature within us all. I have had to look directly at my selfishness—in ways I never did prior to motherhood. I am still "becoming" with you.

Yet I have indeed experienced that love for another person, my child, takes commitment, and "commitment to another person costs us . . . self, but the rewards are great."[12]

We are transformed more into the image of our Lord Jesus. Each child has blossomed into a unique little individual. Our Lord has been glorified through our faithfulness as His servant. Therefore, I say, "Rejoice and be glad!"

─────────── PRAYERS AND ANSWERS ───────────

Give thanks to Jesus that He has allowed you to be a servant to a precious new life, your child.

Pray for the courage and strength to face the continued pruning process as you become more like our servant, Jesus.

Pray for the boldness to give praise and honor to our God when others commend you for the selfless attitude you have shown in giving to your child.

Pray for mothers who have ill or handicapped children.

Give to God any troubles you are dragging along this month.

Give thanks for last month's answered prayers.

"Our life is drawn out to full measure precisely by having to accommodate ourselves to the . . . needs of others to whom we are committed."

James Burtchaell
"In a Family Way"

───

NOTES:
1. Jon Johnston, "Growing Me-ism and Materialism," *Christianity Today*, January 17, 1986, page 16-I.
2. Deborah Insel, *Motherhood: Your First 12 Months* (Washington, D.C.: Acropolis Books Ltd., 1982), pages 124-125.

3. Insel, *Motherhood.*
4. Insel, *Motherhood.*
5. Reprinted from *Between Walden and the Whirlwind* by Jean Fleming, © 1985 by The Navigators. Used by permission of NavPress, Colorado Springs, Colo. All rights reserved. Page 110.
6. James T. Burtchaell, "In a Family Way," *Christianity Today,* June 12, 1987, pages 26-27.
7. From *A Mother's Work* by Deborah Fallows, copyright 1985 by Deborah Fallows. Reprinted by permission of Houghton Mifflin Company. Page 33.
8. Louis Genevie, Ph.D. and Eva Margolies, eds., *The Motherhood Report* (New York: Macmillan Publishing Co., 1987), page 123.
9. Fleming, *Between Walden and the Whirlwind,* page 89.
10. Fleming, *Between Walden and the Whirlwind,* page 89.
11. Dee Jepsen, *Women: Beyond Equal Rights* (Waco, Tex.: Word Books, 1984), page 133.
12. Jepsen, *Women: Beyond Equal Rights,* page 131.

A FRIEND LOVES
AT ALL TIMES

BODY AND MIND

Emily Dickinson, the poet, was correct when she said to a friend in June 1869, "A letter always feels to me like immortality because it is the mind alone without the corporeal friend."

The other day I had a heart-to-heart reunion. My friends and I sat together in a small corner of my storage closet and reminisced for a few hours. After we said our "good-byes," and I closed my file box of letters, I realized how precious each one was. I thanked the Father for the gift of friendship. Each letter had been an affectionate and tender kiss from Him to encourage, challenge, and mature me in my faith. I was grateful that "relationships of the Spirit are forever because of His blood," and "distance, as well as differing personal choices, cannot change this."[1]

Since you have physically and emotionally recovered from your child's birth, and the intensity of your child's needs has waned, a yearning for intimacy with old friends has probably kindled within you. As you seek to renew these friendships, you need to look at them realistically—

in the present, not in the past.

The changes you and I go through when we enter different seasons of life can separate us from our friends. Yet with prayer, patience, and perseverance, the covenant of friendship cannot be ripped apart—even when a major change occurs in the relationship, such as the birth of a baby.

Coping with Changed Relationships

As we examine how the birth of your first child has affected you socially, you need to keep two details in the forefront of your thoughts.

First, keep in mind the definition of the word *friend*. It comes from two Old English words: *freon* and *freo*. *Freon* means to love; and *freo* means to be free. Thus, friend means one who is free to love another.

Second, do not overlook the Source and Center of this freedom. We read in 2 Corinthians 3:17, "The Lord is the Spirit, and where the Spirit of the Lord is, there is freedom." When our friendships are rooted deep in the Lord Jesus, they resemble a triple-braided cord. Ecclesiastes 4:12 says, "A cord of three strands is not quickly broken." If Jesus is the center strand of the cord, nothing can sever these relationships.

With these ideas in mind, you will see how you can be "a friend who loves at all times" while you work through the changes your child's birth brings to your friendships.

In Chapter Seven, we discussed the sacrifices you are making as a new parent. One sacrifice, which directly affects your friendships, is the lack of time you have to socialize. Without enough time to devote to them, your friendships can become strained. Also, you and your friends may now have divergent interests. Or, finances may hinder further development of some friendships.

Your child's birth will affect your relationships with

single friends and childless couples more so than your relationships with friends who are parents. Therefore, you will have to expend more effort to keep these relationships vital. You may want to tell your single and childless friends how much you still value their friendship. Focus on what made you friends in the beginning—the mutual interests and values that enabled your relationship to mature. When you are together, show concern for what is occurring in your friend's life instead of centering the entire conversation on your child.

Perseverance and prayer are necessary to keep your valued friendships present and alive during the early years of parenting. Yet working through life's changes with another person can only draw you closer together.

The day I had the reunion with my "friends," I was reminded of how worthwhile working through various life changes with them had been. With my eyes closed, I saw what my friendships had formed over the years—a rainbow tapestry. All that we had grown through together was interwoven in bold blues and reds, somber grays and browns, highlighted with soft pastels. I also saw that this tapestry was incomplete—still on the loom, waiting for the next changes to add new colors to the pattern.

I hope you see in your life's tapestry friends whose threads are being sewn into your life's design, despite the changes in your lives, lapse of time, or distance between you. Along with this hope, I share a personal exhortation. Do not allow the threads of your tapestry to be tied in a final knot because of your child's birth. Continue to be sensitive to your friends' needs so that the weaving of your tapestry may go on.

In order to be sensitive to your friend's needs, and vice versa, you have to be honest with one another. The Lord gives us freedom to love one another, and love, in this case, means boldness and openness. Ask yourselves what you each need from this friendship, what your short-term and long-term expectations are, and how you can realistically love and encourage one another at this point in your lives.

With your heart firmly committed to working through the changes and being honest about needs, there are ways to keep friendships alive while being a new parent. But before I present suggestions for maintaining friendships, let me remind you that the Spirit of the Lord is the One who keeps friendships woven together. A more profound way for us to view our friends is to recognize that "our commitment to Christ binds us irrevocably together,"[2] and our communion with one another is in and through the Father.

It is also important to recognize that you may not communicate as much as you once did with one another. I realized this as I reread a letter from Ruthie written a few years prior to either of our sons' births. I was put at ease, again, when I saw we both shared the same frustrations and concerns:

> Stephanie. . . . It gets harder and harder to write letters that feel true to my experience. Each day is so full, and it feels so strange not to share details with you. However, communicate we will, the best we can. And the Holy Spirit will do the loving.[3]

The suggestions I offer for maintaining friendships are only suggestions. They are not all inclusive. May the Lord help you as you discover the best methods for keeping your friendships.

- Exchange prayer needs over the phone or through letters. Keep each other informed about the answers.
- Remember days that have special significance—

birthdays, anniversaries, graduations, holidays—to
your friends.
- Write a special monthly letter to your friend.
  Include significant happenings in your family, clip-
  pings of articles you've read that your friend would
  appreciate reading, or other small tokens that show
  your friend how valuable and special she is to you.
- Keep a "friends" file on hand to save specific items
  that would interest them or speak to who they are
  and what they need.

Now let's shift our focus from the "how tos" of friendship to
the "whys." Let's explore why old friends are necessary and
important to you and your husband as new parents.

Why Friendships Are So Important

Intimate friends who have known you for awhile can support
you emotionally. A few weeks before Ruthie had Zachary,
Daniel and I received a special "heart" letter from her. Near
the end, she expressed the goodness of close friends:

> Thanks for letting me spill words on the page and send
> them to you. It is good to have friends I can trust with
> such "spillage."[4]

You and your husband know that marriage is not an
all-sufficient relationship within itself. Especially now with a
baby, your marriage "needs elements of an extended family,
of persons who have covenanted to be available . . . and
sensitive to [y]our needs."[5]

Close friends can also help you overcome the feelings of
isolation you may experience as a new mother. Even though
these friends may be miles away, just knowing that they love
and care for you can be enough. When you do need encour-

agement and a listening heart, they are available via the telephone.

In Chapter Four we discussed a new mother's need to be mothered in the early months following childbirth. A similar need may arise for you in relationship with your friends. This need is for a "ritual homecoming," which is fulfilled when you are a guest in a friend's home. Your husband may receive this homecoming frequently, but you, too, need to receive the "joy of being cared for and fussed over maternally."[6]

Since Asher has become part of our family, I know the delight and rest I've received by having a meal with a friend at her home. I savored every minute—from the conversation, to the food, to no cleanup afterwards. I left her home refreshed.

Most important, your friends are crucial to your continued spiritual growth. God desires us to continue the community of fellowship with our friends. Henri Nouwen, in his book, *Making All Things New*, gives us a good perspective on fellowship:

> The discipline of community makes us persons; that is, people who are sounding through to each other . . . a truth . . . and a love which is greater, fuller, and richer than we ourselves can grasp. In true community we are windows constantly offering each other new views on the mystery of God's presence in our lives.[7]

Finally, as you and your husband seek to work and grow through your social changes, be assured that a Best Friend is always with you—even when your friends cannot be physically present to support you, or when you possibly are struggling to mend the tears in your friendships. Your Friend is Jesus, who loves at all times.

| REFLECTIONS |

Now consider the definition of friend I gave earlier. In the context of your friendships with career mothers and/or "at-home" mothers, think about what it means to be free to love another. In Chapter Six, you were asked to pray for harmony between mothers in differing roles. Consider your role and ask yourself if reconciliation needs to occur between you and any of your friends because of your different choices. Reconciliation can only happen when you both accept each other's role decisions. You must be content with your choice, but not envy your friend's role. Most important, you must have a strong sense of your personal identity so you won't be threatened by each other's choices. The positive outcome of working through this possible problem is a renewed appreciation of what you each can bring to the friendship. You both can wholeheartedly support one another; you are free to love another with the freedom the Spirit of the Lord gives.

When you think about your close friends, what mental images do you see?

List the friends you and your husband recognize as extended family.

Since the birth of your child:

Where have you experienced tugs and tears in your cord of friendships?

What specific ways can you be more sensitive to your friends' needs?

Where have you failed to be honest about your needs and expectations?

How have your friends helped you feel less isolated?

Have you experienced a "ritual homecoming" in a friend's home? If so, describe how you were refreshed.

Do you need to reconcile a friendship? If so, with whom and why?

Describe how Jesus can be your best Friend during your social changes.

─────────────────────┤ HEART AND SPIRIT ├─────────────────────

As we have opportunity, let us do good to all people, especially to those who belong to the family of believers.

Galatians 6:10

In this chapter, we are diverging from the Bible study format we have followed thus far. You are going to put Galatians 6:10 into action and love the friends who have been a part of your life through many changes—especially this last major change, your child's birth.

Your goal this month is to write letters to three friends: a single friend, a married friend without a child, and a married friend with a child. As you are generous with your love through words to your friends, you will receive the promise given in Proverbs 11:25, "A generous man will prosper; he who refreshes others will himself be refreshed."

Before you begin, however, you need to examine the letters of an excellent biblical letter writer so you can learn what to include in your letters. The writer I refer to is the Apostle Paul. In reading through his letters to the churches, it is easy to see that his words resulted from much fervor, passion, and love. He always loved his brothers and sisters deeply, from the heart.

Look up the following verses, and record how Paul's choice of words shows his love for his extended family. Where applicable, record what Paul wanted them to know or what he wanted to give to them.

Romans 1:8-13

2 Corinthians 2:3-4

Philippians 1:2-11, 4:1

1 Thessalonians 2:6-8

2 Timothy 1:3-5

Philemon 4-7

After understanding Paul's heart, ask the Lord to show you who to write and to fill you with the same love Paul had for his friends.

Also, at your leisure, examine Paul's letters more closely (especially Galatians 5:13-14, 6:2; Ephesians 4:2, 29,32; Colossians 3:12-14; 1 Thessalonians 5:11). You will see in these verses how Paul wanted his brothers and sisters in the Lord to love one another. He wanted them to encourage one another, build one another up in the faith, forgive one another, carry each other's burdens, share in each other's troubles, and serve one another in love.

With these ideas in mind from your brother Paul, and with the understanding of how he loved others through his letters, you are ready to begin writing. As you write to your friends, consider each one as a good and perfect gift from our Father.

The outline below shows what Paul tried to include in

his letters. Use or delete what you feel is necessary for you when writing to your friends. Blessed writing to you!

- Open with a greeting in the Lord Jesus.
- Give thanks for who they are as persons.
- Pray for them.
- Encourage them in their faith.
- Ask them their needs and prayer requests.
- Show interest and concern in what they are doing with their life at present.
- Share your personal joys, sorrows, hopes, and needs with them.
- Ask forgiveness, if reconciliation is necessary in any area of your friendship.
- Close with a "thank you" for their continued friendship and constant love during this new season in your life.

PRAYERS AND ANSWERS

Pray that each friend to whom you are writing will receive encouragement and love from the Lord through you.

Pray for the missionary families in your church who need an extended family of friends in the country where they serve.

Pray for the opportunity to give a new mother a "ritual homecoming" in your home.

Ask the Lord to show you specifically where you need to be sensitive to your friends.

Pray that you will let the Lord Jesus be your best Friend during your days of isolation from friends.

Give thanks for the extended family our Lord has given you.

> *Bring me a friend*
> *who cares,*
> *knowing pain and loneliness*
> *and feels its desolation—*
> *who listens and*
> *forfeits condemnation.*
>
> *Show me a friend*
> *who is free*
> *to share my heart's reflections*
> *on life and death and*
> *heaven's mystifying will*
> *and fitful dusky sight.*
>
> *Find me a friend*
> *who's walked*
> *with paradox and contradiction,*
> *who accepts another as he is*
> *and wonders if correctitude*
> *is determined by decree.*
>
> *Lord, create of me*
> *the friend*
> *I long to be.*

Patsie Black
Tapestry: A Finespun Grace and Mercy

NOTES:
1. Excerpt of a personal letter from Ruthie Alig, Fall 1980.
2. Lloyd John Ogilvie, "The Triple-Braided Cord," *The Beauty of Friendship* (Irvine, Calif.: Harvest House Publishers, 1980).

3. Excerpt of a personal letter from Ruthie Alig, February 11, 1982.
4. Excerpt of a personal letter from Ruthie Alig, April 10, 1985.
5. Colleen and Louis Evans, Jr., *Bold Commitment* (Wheaton, Ill.: Victor Books/Scripture Press, 1983), page 96.
6. Kathryn Rabrizzi, *The Sacred and the Feminine: Toward a Theology of Housework* (New York: Seabury Press, 1982), page 96.
7. Henri J.M. Nouwen, *Making All Things New* (San Francisco: Harper & Row, 1981), page 87.

RESTING BETWEEN HIS WINGS

BODY AND MIND

Little Jessica McClure captured the country's attention and hearts overnight. For two days she was the lead story on national television and in newspapers. The nation anxiously awaited her rescue. Then, on the evening of Friday, October 16, 1987, the networks interrupted prime-time television to bring a live news report from Midland, Texas. Eighteen-month-old Jessica, who fell into a narrow, abandoned well behind her home, was soon to be retrieved.

That evening, only a few minutes before the paramedic guided Jessica out on a lift, I had walked into my house and turned on the television. I recalled how I had briefly prayed for her survival on Wednesday and had sighed an "Oh, my!" at the possible tragedy. In my mind, this human drama was only one in many that happens every day, somewhere in the world. *Nothing to get excited or worked up over*, I had said to myself. But the moment I saw her emerge and realized she was still alive—after fifty-eight hours in the well—I began sobbing. I remember saying, "What a miracle! What a mira-

131

cle! Thank you, Lord!"

This same emotional grip of the heart, with tears welling up in my eyes, had occurred before on numerous occasions as I watched near-death situations that involved little children. Yet the intensity of my response had increased since Asher's birth. With each scenario, I thought, *This could have been Asher.*

No doubt you, too, have said a few times, "This could have been." Fears of danger that threaten the health or welfare of your child have probably haunted you at one time or another during the past nine months. And don't think these fears will instantly vanish. As long as you are a parent, you will have to face each fear eye to eye—maybe even with boxing gloves—until you can defeat it. Let prayer be your boxing gloves and the Spirit of the Lord be your hands. You are not expected to defeat this enemy alone.

Please do not misinterpret me. You should be concerned for your child and try to protect him or her. But we each need to be aware that our fears "tempt us to try to control [our children's] environment. Then we limit their experience and growth."[1]

Dealing with Fear

This month is an especially appropriate time to disclose a difficult part of parenting: dealing with your fears for your child. Your child is now in constant motion. In a few months he or she will be toddling around. You can no longer protect your child in your arms. The scope of your child's world grows as he or she does, expanding beyond your control and constant attention. Mishaps become more possible.

With the recognition of how little control you have on your child's well-being as he or she matures, fear becomes a crucial topic to consider. If you do not begin to expose each fear in these early months, you will stockpile them year after year. Your stockpile of fears may fence your child in, causing him or her to lose the time needed for innocence and a carefree spirit. A child who matures within a circle of fear may acquire an unhealthy view of the world. Fear, instead of the Lord's peace, will become your child's constant guide.

Do not think you are all alone with your fears: fears have been with us since the Fall. Although fear is natural, we need to know the godly way to deal with and overcome our fears. Our Lord wants to give us a life of hope and joy—not one of despair and gloom. Fear devours our vitality for life and can keep us from loving our children as we should.

Unfortunately, our society exists in a continual state of fear. This fear is a subtle epidemic to which we often succumb. Just listen to the news each day, or glance at the daily newspaper headlines. What literally sells the news is negativism, wrapped in fear. Since you and I are greatly influenced and often controlled by what we read, hear, and see, our exposure to society's fears warps our minds and emotions. Unnecessary worries invade our thoughts. Let's examine how this fear invasion has affected our generation.

In the September 1, 1986 issue of *Newsweek*, the lead story discussed why many couples are opting not to have children. If you recall, we listed (in Chapter Five) the main reasons couples gave for choosing to be childless. One reason dealt with particular social views, or more precisely, "social fears."

> Couples feel overwhelmed by a world that seems to grow increasingly beyond the control of parents. "Young people today are exposed to more pressures to experiment with drinking, drugs and sex. . . . It's frightening. . . . This world is a crazy place to try and raise a kid. We could well blow ourselves up before the child has a chance to mature."[2]

Wanda Urbanska, in her book *The Singular Generation*, describes this same fear. She uses the word *insecure* to describe why the current generation is concerned about parenting:

> The singular generation is the product of the most turbulent epoch in American history. Born in the late fifties and sixties, we grew up in the sixties, seventies, and eighties, a time in which every given was subject to revision—the sanctity of marriage, the expectation of upward mobility, the military and domestic indomitability of the United States, even the certainty that life on Planet Earth would continue. As a result, the singular generation is the most insecure generation in recent history. . . . Without anything about which to feel secure, the singular generation has had a hard time planting our feet on the ground. At some fundamental level, we have never learned how to trust—in love, in marriage, in children and even in the religious and secular institutions in which our predecessors once laid their faith. . . . The search for strength and security is our central obsession.[3]

Our generation definitely lives, in part, a gloomy existence, without hope to pass on to their children (that is, if they have children). Fear controls many in our generation, and may prevent many couples from investing in the most precious and priceless resource—children.

What other fears, which want to attach themselves to you like a leech, lurk in our society? What about the AIDS epidemic? What about the thousands of missing children? What about child abuse? What about the chance of a nuclear war? What about the possibility of an economic disaster? The list of fears that besiege us goes on.

However, at this point in parenting, these colossal fears are probably not at the top of your list. More than likely your immediate concerns are with "child-proofing" your house or the fear that your child will choke on a small household item or a piece of food. You may also wonder if your child is being neglected at the daycare center. Perhaps you feel insecure about leaving your child with a particular babysitter. Or perhaps you are afraid that you or your husband will forget to close the gate at the staircase.

You need to look at your list of fears, which has already begun to grow, and find the taproot. For your fears will not decrease, but will increase as your child matures and moves further from your world.

The Ultimate Fear

Reflect for a moment on the fears described in the discussion about our society. In all honesty, what would you say is the dominant fear that gives life to all the other fears?

The answer, of course, is death. Death is the taproot of all fears. If this worst and most horrible fear is also yours, you are not alone. Many fears that you and I as mothers may be anxious about are petty, but death is catastrophic. You and I know that to love our child is to know how much pain and hurt would encompass us if we were to lose this precious life. Mike Mason, in his book *The Mystery of Marriage*, writes about death, the ultimate fear we have as parents:

> If it is true that marriage intensifies the darkness of death's shadow, then surely having a child makes it darker still. The threat, the risk, the potential for tragedy are tripled when shared three ways. . . . And what is more devastating or incomprehensible than the death of a child? And is not the loss of a loved child felt as a much greater tragedy than the death of an orphan?

A family knows all this instinctively, and that is why there is no individual, no unit, no other organization on earth that is more protective of human life, and so more agonized by death, than the family.[4]

In facing your worst fear, and mine, too, I do not want to be morbid or ask you to prepare for the death of your child, then hope for the best. Our Lord knows all too well the immense agony we feel with the loss of a beloved child. He also knows that when you love deeply, you hurt deeply. So I only ask you to face this taproot fear head-on—not alone, but with the help of our loving Father. For if you fail to acknowledge this fear now, and whenever it recurs, your fear will become a noose around your child's neck.

None of us knows the dangers our children will encounter, but we do know the Father and Creator of the universe, who carries our children in the palm of His hand. If He cradles them, He is ultimately responsible for their well-being.

As you ponder the following quote, know that our Lord also holds you in His hand. He understands your fears. So, dear one, rest between His shoulders; let Him give you a heart and mind of peace.

> Our children never really belong to us. They are God's from the beginning and only loaned to us for whatever length of time and whatever eternal purpose God has in mind. And yet, they are truly a part of our very life and being. . . . Only trusting that God is their true source and true ending can bring any peace of mind.[5]

Now that you have begun to discern your fears as a new mother, thoughtfully consider the following questions. Be honest with yourself and our Lord in your answers.

| REFLECTIONS |

During the last nine months, what fears have you had for your child?

Are these fears still cluttering your mind and heart? If so, which ones do you need the Lord to help you dismiss?

How have you succumbed to the fears perpetuated by the media?

Write down any fears you have allowed to warp the perception our Lord wants you to have about life.

In thinking about death, the taproot fear, what will our Lord need to do in your life so that you will not allow this fear to rule the way you raise your child or to rob you of peace?

| HEART AND SPIRIT |

In the psalms of David, we find a wellspring of encouragement and comfort. Here we see another human being who
captures in words the aches and fears of our hearts and turns
them into supplications to our Father.

We also discover the imagery with which David describes our Lord. Two images that we need to look at in
particular this month are those that describe our Father as a
protector and a giver of rest.

Look up the following verses from the Psalms, and write
down the images of protection David addresses to the Lord.
In each verse also note what the Lord is likened to, how He
protects, and how to find rest from your fears.

Psalm 17:6-9

Psalm 36:5-7

Psalm 57:1-2

Psalm 63:6-8

Psalm 91:1-4

As you can see from these psalms, our rest and protection comes from abiding, in faith, under the wings of the Lord God. The image of a majestic bird, which David ascribes to the Lord, is a very comforting and consoling one. The wings of a bird, especially those of a large one, are designed to hide the offspring from predators. Even the downy feathers, located near the tail, are so fluffy that they aid in protection.

God promises to protect and comfort you—one of His precious children—under His wings. So when fears do threaten to snatch you from His protection and comfort, look to David's words to give you rest:

> When I am afraid,
>   I will trust in you.
> In God, whose word I praise,
>   in God I trust; I will not be afraid.
>   What can mortal man do to me?
>
> Psalm 56:3-4

Now we need to take our study one step beyond recognizing and acknowledging the One who gives us protection and rest. Rest and protection cannot come unless we allow God to give them to us. But in order to receive these gifts, we first must confess our fears and understand who is the author of fear.

1. Read 1 Peter 5:7-9 and 1 John 4:15-18. In your own words, write out what your responsibility is in regard to your fears. Define what you must acknowledge and be aware of.

In the previous section, we shared that the worries you have for your child will not disappear on their own. To conquer these fears, you must look directly at them and fight them off with God's assistance.

2. In Ephesians 6:10-17 we are told who we battle against and how to equip ourselves for the fight.

a. As you read this passage, write down specifically what you are required to put on. Then envision how it would help you to be clothed in each piece.

b. After you have dressed yourself in God's armor, what two important things does verse 18 instruct you to do?

c. Why are these instructions important in facing your fears? (One is the same as in 1 Peter 5:8.)

3. Read Philippians 4:6.

a. What are you to do with your anxieties?

b. The action requested here is the same as in the previous verses we have studied, yet this verse tells you how to perform this action. What new emphasis does this verse present?

c. Why is this particularly important when giving your anxieties about your child's welfare to God?

When we present our needs and deepest fears to God, with thanksgiving, we must believe He will meet our needs and erase our fears. In faith, we can thank Him for answering our prayers even before we see the results.

4. Philippians 4:7 is a promise that is fulfilled as we give thanks and trust in the Lord's care and protection. Write down what the Lord will give to you and do for you when you give Him your fears.

You are His child, young mother—guarded and protected under the wings of His care. Know that the following words from the Old Testament are eternally true. They apply to you now and always as you continue your journey of motherhood:

> "Let the beloved of the LORD rest secure in him,
>   for he shields him all day long,
>   and the one the LORD loves rests between his
>   shoulders."
>
> Deuteronomy 33:12

PRAYERS AND ANSWERS

Give our Lord each specific fear you have regarding your child.

Pray for the parents you know who have had a child die.

Pray for the Lord to guard your heart and mind from the Devil's subtle schemes, since he will try to invade your life with fears.

Pray for the opportunity to minister words of comfort and life to a mother whose fears control her actions toward her child.

Give thanks for the Lord's peace and freedom from fear.

"From the moment we awake until we fall asleep, we must commend our loved ones wholly and unreservedly to God and leave them in his hands, transforming our anxiety then into prayers on their behalf."

Dietrich Bonhoeffer
Letters and Papers from Prison

NOTES:
1. Taken from *Learning to Let Go* by Carol Kuykendall, copyright 1985 by Carol Kuykendall. Used by permission of Zondervan Publishing Company. Page 59.
2. "Three's a Crowd," *Newsweek*, September 1, 1986, page 20.
3. Wanda Urbanska, *The Singular Generation* (Garden City, N.Y.: Doubleday, 1986), pages 1-2.
4. Mike Mason, *The Mystery of Marriage* (Portland, Oreg.: Multnomah Press, 1985), page 173.
5. Kuykendall, *Learning to Let Go*, page 58.

LIKE A LITTLE CHILD

Not far from our house, there is a large park where people of all ages gather to enjoy the pleasure of being outdoors. One corner of the park is equipped for little children. Here they have a sandbox, swings, a Cinderella pumpkin carriage, and rocking horses. I drive by this corner of the park frequently. When the weather permits, children, mothers, and fathers are nearly always playing together there.

For a long time, I took this scene for granted; it seemed so common to see children and families in a park. But as Zachary neared ten months of age, I began to think about taking him to the park. *Maybe he would enjoy the baby swings and the pumpkin ride,* I thought, and perhaps I would even enjoy the park, too.

Although common at first glance, the activities that go on at the park symbolize for me the special roles new mothers add to their repertoire as they approach the tenth month of their first year of motherhood. Imagine for a moment a mother holding her baby while they swing and laugh. See her point to a tree, look her child in the face, and say, "tree." See her watch other mothers and children, even as her baby watches them. Playing, learning, and socializing all go on at the park, and a child at ten months relies on his or her mother in all these pursuits—in the park and elsewhere.

You have already discovered that being a mother draws on all of your personal resources—body, mind, heart, and spirit. Through your commitment and love, you have helped your child grow through the early months of total dependence, providing food, comfort, rest, and stimulation. Now, as you near the completion of your first year as a mother, your baby's needs are expanding. The small bundle given to you ten months ago is ready for action, and you are the nearest, most dependable source of action.

You and your child are now entering a world of multiple demands and plentiful joys. Your child wants to interact with the surrounding world, and you are his or her bridge to new wonders. In addition to the roles you already fulfill, you will be called upon to be a playmate and a teacher. As your child's bridge to the world, you are the one who introduces new people, helping your child learn how to socialize. So this month we will consider your role in play, learning, and socialization.

Play—For You and Your Child

Let us first explore the realm of play. Child development experts have written many books on the value of play in a child's life. Maria Piers and Genevieve Millet Landau, authors of *The Gift of Play: And Why Young Children Cannot Thrive Without It*, write, "Play is not merely the child's way of learning, it is the only good and lasting way of learning for the young child. Through play children learn and polish skills— social, emotional, physical, mental."[1]

You have been playing with your child since birth—

snuggling, cooing, bouncing. In many ways, you know instinctively what your baby will enjoy at different stages of development. If you run short on ideas, you can always seek new information at the library, a bookstore, or by talking with other mothers.

But this book is not so much a study of what babies need for development as it is a book about your development. Of course play is vital for your baby, but the question we need to address is, how do you feel about playing? Is play only for the baby or is there genuine play on your part as well? What are the joys and frustrations of being an adult with an infant playmate? Is play an art that can be improved with practice and imagination?

I became sensitive to the significance of play when I was nineteen years old. I had been a baby-sitter for many years and by age nineteen was able to verbalize some of the nagging fears I had about playing with children. This portion from my journal was written after spending a day caring for a baby who was about ten months old:

> I have an inner fear of never caring for children. Having children does not bother me as much as my feelings about spending time with them. I am scared of them because I can't communicate on my level with them and because I don't understand them.
>
> I am very self-centered around children, finding it hard to put aside my interests for their needs. I can't entertain them comfortably; I am usually bored or ill-at-ease.

As I read these words from my past, I see that I was yearning to be able to play with a child in a way that was fulfilling for both of us. I was reaching out for help—perhaps anticipating the time when I would be a mother—and wanting so dearly not to be unwilling to play with my child when called upon.

During my brief time as a mother, I have observed some qualities of play that both encourage and challenge me. Of course my observations are shaped by my personality, but perhaps you can find some ideas that you can adapt to your own style of play.

First, I observed that the rewards for playing with my child are great. Seeing my son respond as he discovers a new object, skill, or concept is an unparalleled thrill. His delight and growing confidence motivate me to continue to play.

Conversely, during the tedious times when my child wants to play a game for the "hundredth" time, or I'm too tired to be excited, or I'd rather read a novel, I have no easy answers. I'm not very good at faking enjoyment, so I have to choose whether I will play without enthusiasm or if it would be better to refuse to play and turn his attention to some other activity.

To avoid an abundance of tedious times, I have found it helpful to sometimes involve the baby in play that is challenging to me. If my imagination and sense of play is stimulated, my resources for playing with my child expand, and we're both happier. I then have more energy and willingness to play on his level.

For example, I love to dance. Sharing music and dance with Zachary has been a great source of play for both of us. We also like to visit museums and toy stores together. I try to find children's books with beautiful illustrations so that my eyes are pleased, as well as his. I also watch his Pappa play with him and learn new ways to play. These pleasures feed my desire to play.

What special play interests do you have? Think about the activities you enjoy most and determine which ones can be shared with your child.

Sometimes, Zachary and I need to play in different ways. I have discovered that taking time for grown-up play, without Zachary, has been important for me as a mother. Spending time with my husband, a friend, or alone, has greatly improved my attitude toward playing with my child.

I have special memories of a day when a friend and I both hired baby-sitters and treated ourselves to an elegant lunch at a downtown restaurant. Afterwards we browsed through shops, unencumbered by strollers and diaper bags. We thoroughly enjoyed this grown-up play, and we returned to our children with a greater enthusiasm for mothering.

Play is not a waste of time. Those who shun or downgrade play are missing out on a great adventure. As Frank and Theresa Caplan say in *The Power of Play*:

> Man as an artist is infinitely more ancient than man as a worker. Man has made his greatest progress when not grubbing for necessities, when nature was so bountiful that he had the leisure to play and the inclination to tinker. It is the child in man that is the source of his creativeness.[2]

Perhaps we mothers, who are the people most free to participate in play, are thereby blessed with the ability to become genuinely creative. Our play adventures may be discernible only to us as a busy world passes us by, but we are building joy for our children and for ourselves that will be visible in everything we do.

The Playmate as Teacher

Inextricably bound to the role of playmate is the role of teacher, since almost all teaching at this age is done through play. As your child's playmate, you are a wellspring of information, sharing your knowledge of creation with your child. You are wonderfully skilled at distilling facts into a form that is meaningful for your child. Your daily actions are filled with teaching power as your baby observes the rituals of life and learns to imitate you.

But we mothers need to be careful about taking our teaching role to an extreme. In a highly competitive and technological society, we may drive our child to learn faster than he or she is ready. *Newsweek*, in an article titled "Kids Need Time to Be Kids," discusses how early childhood specialists are encouraging parents to de-emphasize formal instruction for very young children in favor of giving children plenty of time to play. The writers conclude, "Childhood is over quickly enough, and allowing children to learn at their own pace may be the most lasting gift parents can give their young."[3] We need to check ourselves to ensure that we are not pressuring our child to learn, even though our intentions of helping the child to succeed are good.

Our role as teacher also encompasses the spiritual dimension of our child's development.

You may wonder what you could possibly be teaching your child about spiritual life at ten months of age, when in fact you are your child's first experience of God's love. Through your consistent love and care, you have set your baby free to trust and love others. You are your child's bridge to God through all the playing and teaching you share with him or her in these early years (and through your prayers of intercession for your child).

In short, you are vital to your child's spiritual formation—even at this early age. Thus, it is all the more important for you to remain in close communion with God. During these early months, you are getting to know your child as the unique person he or she is. This knowledge will give you a context from which you can serve and instruct your child in the years ahead.

The Complexities of Comparison

In the park, at church, at the daycare center, or wherever children gather, you will meet other mothers. As your child learns social skills, you will learn things about yourself as well.

In social settings where young children and their mothers gather, comparisons take place. You will find yourself comparing your actions to those of other mothers and comparing your baby to other babies. And you can be sure other mothers are doing the same. For instance, I rarely, if ever, paid attention to young mothers in relationship to their babies before Zachary was born. But after his birth—what a difference! I watched other mothers with awe and respect, especially those with more than one child.

I also experienced a growing urge to size up another mother and compare myself to her. Sometimes I'd see a mother who seemed so much more adequate than myself, so peaceful and efficient in her role. Then I'd see one who seemed slack, barely holding things together. Or I'd judge a mother for being too pushy or too restrictive.

Why did I make such critical observations about mothers? I believe it was because of the newness of my experience and my insecurity from knowing so little about who I was as a mother. Comparisons may help a new mother form a clearer picture of herself, but if taken too far, she may never gain confidence or learn to accept different styles of mothering.

The challenge for us as new mothers is to be at peace with ourselves as we develop our own styles of mothering. We can learn from each other without tearing ourselves or each other down. William Hulme, in his book *Firstborn*, gives this encouragement: "If you can accept your imperfection, you can learn to be content . . . to let others be . . . to enjoy rather than defend."[4]

In conjunction with the temptation to compare yourself to other mothers, there is the just-as-frequent desire to compare your child with others. Some of the same principles apply to both types of comparisons. It's difficult not to compare your child to others when you're so involved and want so badly to know that he or she is doing well. Some critical discernment is spontaneous and natural because you're beginning to see your child's uniqueness, but some judgments are potentially destructive.

As you observe your child's personality, skills, growth, and appearance in a social context, think about your feelings. Are you content to let your child be his or her own unique person, or are you uncomfortable with your child's development in comparison to others?

We may feel that our children reflect how successful or unsuccessful we are as mothers. This attitude, if extreme, places a heavy burden on the child to fit our image of successful mothering. Again, these comparisons stem from our insecurity, so we must be conscious of any such extremes. As we seek a less competitive attitude, our children will be free to be their unique selves.

As your child's social world expands, you or your baby may be on the receiving end of comparative or critical statements by others. New mothers commonly hear comments like, "Don't you make him eat his vegetables?" "Is he still using a bottle?" "He doesn't smile much, does he?" or, "Gosh, you're a big baby!" We can tolerate such observations better if we have established some security in our role as mothers. Also, people are generally positive toward babies and their mothers, and being a part of society can be a great source of joy. We, too, can create joy for others when we remember to make encouraging comments to mothers, both about them and about their children.

In exciting and vital ways, you are your child's bridge to

new wonders. Next time you drive by a park where children and mothers are playing, remember your personal development as a human being and rejoice in the gifts of play, teaching, and community that God has brought into your life. May God bless you with inner security and joy, this month and always.

———————————| REFLECTIONS |———————————

Describe a time recently when you enjoyed playing with your child.

What play activities bring you pleasure? Of these, which ones can be shared with your child and which ones are only for you?

How has teaching your child about the world around her or him made you more aware of how much knowledge you can share?

What is your favorite way of teaching your child something new?

What type of mother is particularly difficult for you to be around? What do you think is the root cause for your discomfort?

Are you pushing your child in any way as a result of comparing him or her to others?

How do you support the uniqueness of your child? How do you support your own uniqueness?

Write down a negative comment someone made about your child. How did you feel inside?

Now write down a positive comment someone made about your child and how you responded to it.

Record any further reflections you have about this month. What problems or concerns not mentioned this month are real for you?

──────────────┤ HEART AND SPIRIT ├──────────────

1. Read Mark 10:13-16, and write out the verses in your own words.

2. What are Jesus' physical actions toward children?

3. What three characteristics of little children do you believe Jesus was thinking of when He said, "Receive the kingdom of God like a little child" (verse 15)?

Little children are unable to care for themselves or get what they want on their own. Jesus teaches His disciples in this passage that people cannot enter the Kingdom of God through strength, ability, or merit. The Kingdom is a gift from God, given lovingly to the helpless.

4. Although dependent on you, children respond with joy as you play with and teach them. You are giving them gifts of love. What have you learned since becoming a mother about being "like a little child"?

The gospels record how Jesus taught His disciples about God and His Kingdom. He chose twelve men to be with Him daily during His ministry on earth. He was available to them always, showing them how to live by His example and speech. As a mother, you are with your child on a daily basis and have numerous opportunities to teach your child about life. As Jesus is our bridge to God, you are your child's bridge to knowledge, the world, and faith.

5. Read 2 Timothy 1:3-5. What does Paul say first belonged to Timothy's grandmother and mother and now belongs to Timothy?

6. These verses are Paul's expression of thanksgiving for Timothy's sincere faith in Christ. How do you believe your faith is influencing the development of your child's faith at the present time?

Your child will see, even at this early age, how you relate to other people and will begin to model your behavior. Scripture encourages us to not be competitive or judgmental with others, but to build others up.

7. Write a brief prayer of faith for your ten-month-old child.

8. Read Ephesians 4:29 (also Romans 14:19; 15:2-3,7; 1 Thessalonians 5:11). What should the purpose of our words and actions toward others be, according to these verses?

9. Do these verses also apply to how we treat our children? If so, describe a specific way you could edify your ten-month-old child.

---------------| PRAYERS AND ANSWERS |---------------

What are your prayers for yourself and your child this month?

How has God responded to your earlier prayers?

Pray, by name, for other young mothers you know.

Praise God for the freedom to play with your child.

Pray for God's saving care to be with abused mothers and their children.

"*Consider the play of the child, and the nature of the Kingdom will be revealed. Christ is that fiddler who plays so sweetly that all who hear him begin to dance. But those who prefer to be deaf and know nothing of music will perceive him as a madman and view the dancers as senseless and in bad taste.*"

Robert E. Neale
In Praise of Play

NOTES:
1. Maria Piers and Genevieve Millet Landau, *The Gift of Play: And Why Young Children Cannot Thrive Without It* (New York: Walker and Co., 1980), page 16.
2. Frank and Theresa Caplan, *The Power of Play* (New York: Anchor Press/ Doubleday, 1973), page XX.
3. "Kids Need Time to Be Kids," *Newsweek*, February 2, 1987, page 58.
4. William Hulme, *Firstborn* (St. Louis: Concordia, 1972), page 18.

FACING THE MIRROR

Rushing through a shopping mall, focusing intently on my errands, I suddenly catch a glimpse of myself in a mirror. Self-consciousness takes over. *Why don't I ever take more time to dress decently?* I think. *What are my hips doing way out there? After all, it's been eleven months since Zach was born!* The mirror, now fifty yards behind me, continues to agitate and distract me. How can it do that?

Mirrors evoke both fascination and frustration. Myths, fantasies, and countless stories have explored the relationship of man to mirror. Our image reflected in the mirror has the power to disarm and mystify us.

Some mirrors are merciless as they reflect an image that seems so imperfect. But I doubt that we would want to give up mirror gazing entirely. We are, to some degree, dependent on mirrors to give us security about our appearance and identity.

A mirror, however, reveals only a superficial picture of ourselves. God alone can open our eyes to enable us to see

161

who we really are. When we gaze into His Word, He reflects back a realistic image of ourselves. We can see our brokenness apart from Him and the beautiful, redeemed persons we can become through faith in Jesus Christ. God's love for us helps us see our souls with clear vision and hope.

But there are other mirrors in our lives, too. As a new mother, you have steadily faced a mirror for eleven months now. God has given you a mirror in the form of a child. In his or her physical appearance and personality, your child is a combined image of you and your husband. But this little person also reflects a picture of your soul.

Having a baby has forced you to see yourself clearly. The images you see may be familiar or new to you. Your child is a mirror that reveals your strengths and weaknesses, leading you toward maturity. You would have missed out on so much if you had refused to look into the mirror of your child. But now you have seen yourself more fully and have matured as a woman.

Facing the Reality of Values

This month, we will see how your child reflects your behavioral, financial, ethical, and spiritual values. We will also peer into your values of discipline. So come, stand with me before the mirror and take a look.

What does a value look like? Huber and Shirley Walsh, in *The First Years of Parenting*, describe a value as "a principle or standard which is made a part of one's code of living. Its roots are tied to something very near and dear to us, something about which we have very definite feelings and thoughts, as we often do on matters such as religion, sexuality, family traditions, responsibility, and so on."[1]

You, of course, had values before your child was born. But the realization that your values will directly and visibly affect your child causes you to scrutinize them more than ever before. Although many of our values are challenged and refined through our becoming parents, we will only discuss a few general values in this chapter; values that are relevant for the eleven-month-old mother.

On a nitty-gritty level, we have behavioral values that are demonstrated in how we eat, dress, and watch television. Our behavior is a visible sign of what we truly value. That which makes us lose our temper or laugh with delight indicates what we value. Our behavior can be imitated by a child, and it is often shocking or surprising to see ourselves reflected in the actions of our children.

As a new mother, your financial values are constantly challenged. You must ask yourself how many toys to buy, what kind of clothes to purchase, and how elaborately to decorate the nursery. Your values shape the decisions you make.

Your ethical values may not be easily observed by an eleven-month-old child, but it won't be long before your ethics will be reflected back to you by your child's choices. Do you lie, or tell the truth? Do you treat others with fairness and mercy? Do you abuse the environment, or try your best to preserve it?

I find it difficult, and perhaps incorrect, to separate values into distinct categories. They all overlap, and our desire as Christians is to see our spiritual values mesh with— and determine—all our other values.

Our spiritual values are seen in part as we choose to pray or not to pray, in our attitude toward worship, in our church involvement, and in our efforts to let the world know Christ's love. Spiritual values are tested in our home life for their consistency and authenticity.

What values do you see in yourself as you look in the mirror? Penelope Washbourn, in her book, *Becoming Woman: The Quest for Wholeness in Female Experience*, addresses children as mirrors: "You have the power to destroy all falsity and reduce us to see us as we are, humble us to see ourselves with all our superficial masks torn away! The sight is painful."[2] But the sight is also a gift of reality. Our child can help us be more honest and inspire us to have greater integrity.

Where do our values come from? We inherit many values from our parents; you are a mirror of them. But you have probably rejected or modified some of your parents' values to fit your generation and personality. Perhaps you have even chosen values that are quite opposite to those of your parents. Your husband has also introduced his values into your life, and together you are developing a family value system.

This meshing of values is not always easy. When it comes to disciplining your child, you can begin to see the process of establishing values that work for both you and your husband.

The Value of Discipline

When Zachary learned to stand up, at about ten or eleven months of age, I had to discipline him for the first time.

He stood in front of the television, turning it on and off repeatedly. "No," I told him and moved him away.

Repeat.

Then, when he showed no obedience, I smacked his hand and moved him away from the television again. The allure of the television was winning, however, and I was feeling horrible with this first direct contact with my son's strong, opposing will.

In walked Pappa. "NO!" he boomed, in his preacher voice, and Zachary literally crumpled at his feet. To this day, Zachary doesn't touch the television without permission.

My husband, my son, and I were new at this discipline business, and we were trying our best to figure it out. Developing a mutual style of discipline with your husband may take a while, and your discipline style will be unique to your family.

In discipline, the values you and your husband have chosen to live by come into action as you set boundaries to keep your child safe and secure and to teach respect for authority at home and in society. In partnership with your husband, you are seeking to discipline with unity, consistency, love, and a vision for the future.

How can two people from different families be unified in their discipline style? It is not easy, but it is worth working on, both for the sake of your relationship with your husband and for your child's well-being.

As a parenting team, you need to respect one another's authority in the home and not put the opinions of your parents or other relatives above your partner's. Relatives may try to impose their values on your child, disciplining in a way contrary to your own. When discipline involves an issue of great importance to you and your husband, you must firmly and lovingly remind the relative that you are in charge.

Life situations will force you and your husband to confront your differences on discipline daily. For the sake of unity, listen to each other and attempt to work out a discipline plan that is acceptable to both of you.

Consistency in discipline is vital. Your child needs to be sure that your "no" means "no," and your "yes" means "yes." Consistency gives a child security. Maintaining consistency between two people is tough, but possible. It is important to keep your husband aware of how you have disciplined your child so he can reinforce what you are doing, and vice versa.

Discipline is an act of love; it is not a synonym for punishment. Discipline is the setting of boundaries that will keep your child safe and secure, and the enforcing of those boundaries as they are transgressed. Discipline affirms the child's self-worth.

Think through for yourself and discuss with your husband these questions about love and discipline:

- What kind of discipline shows the child love?
- When is it time to show the child affection and forgiveness in relation to discipline?
- How can you be sure that your motive for discipline is love?

You and your husband are partners with a vision for your child. You are only just beginning a task that will grow more complex as the child matures. These are foundational days for you as parents, and for your child. One day in the future, your child—prepared by your discipline—will step out into the world, trusting in his or her own inner discipline.

As Hebrews 12:11 says, "No discipline seems pleasant at the time, but painful. Later on, however, it produces a harvest of righteousness and peace for those who have been trained by it." You are building a peaceful adulthood for your child as you seek to discipline him or her with love.

I am very conscious of how incomplete my discussion of discipline appears. I trust that you know there is much more to learn in this area than I could ever discuss. My main hope is to illuminate how values are deeply at work as you discipline your child, and to identify with you and your husband as you work through conflicts while developing your own discipline style. You will make mistakes as you discipline your child, but perfection is not a requirement for parenthood. You must continue to discipline your child, though, learning from each experience.

A mirror shows our imperfections, but the mirror of a

child's loving face shines through all our flaws and assures us that being a mother is a wonderful gift.

———————————— REFLECTIONS ————————————

Name five values you would like to pass on to your child.

In what ways are your values like those of your parents? In what ways do they differ?

In what ways are your values like your husband's? In what ways do they differ?

What strengths and weaknesses do you see in your discipline style?

What further reflections do you have about this eleventh month?

──────────┤ HEART AND SPIRIT ├──────────

The book of James is traditionally considered to have been authored by James, the brother of Jesus. James was regarded as the head of the early Church in Jerusalem (see Acts 15:13).

James wrote his epistle to warn Christians against contradicting in practice what they profess to believe, and to encourage them to always look to Christ—the perfection of the Law—as they make their way through life.

In a sense, the book of James was a mirror by which the early Christians could see themselves more accurately. James wanted to protect them from living an illusion.

1. Read carefully and write out James 1:22-25.

2. What does verse 22 say to you about your values in relationship to hearing and doing?

3. When a Christian ignores the Word of God and acts without regard for it, what happens to the memory of his "face in a mirror"? (See verses 23-24.)

Forgetting what you look like is an illustration of losing one's true identity. If you confront your image in a mirror, you will be forced to see the contradictions between words and actions in your life.

4. According to verse 25, what should a Christian man or woman look into intently?

5. What or who is "the perfect law that gives freedom"?

The "perfect law" referred to here relates to a personal being. It is a biblical concept to understand that Christ is the perfection of the Law as love.

170 / Month Eleven

6.   a. For the person who keeps looking to Christ, both hearing and doing His will, what does verse 25 promise?

   b. As a parent, you have hope that your values will be transformed and made perfect only as you keep your entire being focused on Jesus Christ. But perfection is not a requirement for parenthood. What if you make mistakes or intentionally disobey God's Word? What if guilt is accumulating in your heart?

7. Pray aloud Psalm 139:23-24. Wait in silence for any offenses to become clear to you and write them out below.

The anxious thoughts you have expressed have been made visible to you, as a "mirror" reflecting your soul. Once you face them and ask for Christ's forgiveness and guidance, His light will lead you in "the way everlasting." Keep on looking into Christ, who will lovingly lead you into maturity, so that you will be both a hearer and a doer of the Word—as a mother and as a human being.

| PRAYERS AND ANSWERS |

What concerns are on your heart for you and your child this month?

Pray about specific value changes you would like to see occur in your life.

Pray for God to give you and your husband wisdom to know how to best discipline your child.

Think about the good things God has shown you this month as a mother. Give thanks.

"The family is a sort of crucible in which human beings coalesce, separate, reform in a different way, and spark off diversified reactions. The crucible holds danger certainly, but also, for both parents, a quite incredible fascination and promise as they share in the ultimate creative processes."

Sheila Kitzinger
Women as Mothers

NOTES:
1. Huber and Shirley Walsh, *The First Years of Parenting* (Crawfordsville, Ind.: Presbyterian Church in the United States, 1979), page 27.
2. Penelope Washbourn, *Becoming Woman: The Quest for Wholeness in Female Experience* (San Francisco: Harper & Row, 1977), page 125.

AT THE MILESTONE

Happy "first" birthday! Remembering those early months, when one day merged into the next without distinction, you may be amazed that a year has almost passed. As you approach the milestone this month, take time to look back at your first year as a mother.

Flipping through the pages of your journey as recorded in this book, what major issues have you wrestled with each month—physically, mentally, emotionally, and spiritually? How have you seen God's presence with you in your struggles? What new godly characteristics has He formed in you?

Now travel back to *that* day—the day your child was born. What thoughts swirled in your head during the hours preceding delivery? How was God present with you then? How is He present now? Are there any similarities?

The day Asher was born will always be imprinted on my mind. On the eve of Asher's first birthday, I continually glanced at the clock, vividly recalling every detail of that day a year earlier.

My water broke at 11:45 a.m. Daniel and I were in the car on the way to complete our baby's layette; the baby was not due for five more days. At my request, Daniel continued shopping while I sat trickling in the car.

Before returning home, I deliberately disobeyed the rule of not eating once labor begins. I satisfied my hunger and craving by enjoying a frozen yogurt cone. Licking each bite, I knew real cuisine was a distant reality.

When we arrived home, Daniel called the doctor while I waited in the bathroom. The doctor said to come directly to his office and be ready to go to the hospital. We looked at each other with that knowing grin; our lives would never be the same.

From the time I entered the hospital until seventeen hours later, when Asher Michael made us into a family, I experienced God's peace and presence. His servants were with me during my labor and delivery—my doctor and nurse were both Christians. Before leaving the delivery room, my doctor prayed for us. Fear never overcame me.

Now I know the Lord has been with me every day of Asher's first year. No, I have not always had peace or sensed God's presence the way I did the day Asher was born. At times fear has come, but a growing trust in and dependence on the Lord has been occurring within me—and hopefully within you. Faith has replaced my fear.

This past year, you have been learning to rest in Jesus, allowing Him to show you how to care for your child. From those first awkward, clumsy days when you learned to bathe, burp, and change your child, you have had to depend on Him to build your confidence. Now you must depend on Him as you enter another stage in your development as a mother.

A marvelous phenomenon has been occurring between you and your child since the day he or she was born. You have watched your child grow from a helpless infant to a unique little person who is now an intimate part of your family. You respond to this physical and mental development of your child through a weaning process of your own.

Granted, you are completing, or have completed, your child's weaning. Also, you have continued to gain more independence as your child has developed. These two events have come because of a transition—the shift from bringing your child into the world to releasing him or her into the world.

From now on, each milestone ahead revolves around this weaning or releasing process, which will not be as easy or quick as the physical weaning. Chuck Swindoll speaks of this process in his Bible study guide, *You and Your Child*:

> Begin this process of letting go the day your child is born. Anticipate it. Plan for it. . . . A by-product of preparing children for the seasons and weight of adult life is that the parents themselves become prepared for their release in the process.[1]

Part of your responsibility in this process lies in discerning your child's readiness to take the next developmental step toward independence from you. In recognizing your child's developmental needs, you are recognizing who God has created him or her to be. You are to draw out this unique character instead of molding your child into your design or dreams. Chuck Swindoll offers wise advice on this particular responsibility:

> The first reason for difficulty in releasing children is when parents build themselves into their children rather than developing the children according to how God designed them. Fathers and mothers alike are sometimes guilty of reliving their lives through their

children. Often their motives are good—an "if-I-had-it-all-to-do-over-again" approach. So they try to fill up in their children's lives what was lacking in their own childhood experience. In doing so, a measure of their identity and their dreams is passed on to the children. Consequently, when they leave, a part of the parent leaves with them. And the withdrawal pains can be excruciating.[2]

The major responsibility for you now is to acknowledge who your child belongs to—the Lord Jesus. Psalm 127:3 (NASB) reads, "Children are a gift of the LORD." The Hebrew word for *gift* means property or possession. Therefore, your child is God's property who He has entrusted to you. You are the caretaker.

A week after her son was born, Sandra Bernlehr Clark wrote about her sobering experience of realizing her true role as a mother. The following is an excerpt from her article, "Can My Love Protect My Child?":

The fringe of eyelash. The slight breath. The faint smell of baby powder. Suddenly I am overwhelmed with maternal affection. My throat aches. I hug him tightly. A salty tear spills out of my eye, runs down my cheek, and splashes on the unwitting dreamer. I can taste sadness.

For suddenly I realize that the sheer intensity of my love cannot protect this child from the perils of life. Spinal meningitis. Playground tragedies. Traffic accidents. *God I can't stand it.* My chest constricts with unborn grief. My breath comes quickly. To risk love is to risk loss. Shadows stretch across the living room—and across my mind.

And then I hear it. The still, small voice saying

gently, deep inside, "You're *not* a proud new owner. You're a trusted caretaker. This is my child, and I've lent him to you. Love him dearly, but hold him freely. Trust me for the days ahead."[3]

So as you reach the first milestone of your mothering journey and start for the second, remember that the Lord has been with you from the beginning. Know that He will continue with you in the days ahead. Trust Him with the gift He has given you. And remember to love your child dearly, but to hold him or her freely. You are only the caretaker.

──────────────┤ REFLECTIONS ├──────────────

As you think about your first year as a mother, write down your first feelings or ideas of what you thought mothering would be and what it has really been.

What godly characteristics have formed within you during the past year?

What are three issues you have wrestled with as a new mother?

How have you resolved, or are you resolving, these struggles?

In which areas are you having difficulty releasing your child into God's sovereign care?

List three of the greatest joys you have experienced during your first year of motherhood.

HEART AND SPIRIT

1. Read 2 Thessalonians 2:16-17, and write it out in the space below.

The Scripture passage you wrote has been our prayer and desire for you as you journeyed through your first year of motherhood.

2. As you reflected on the last year, how did you recall the Lord encouraging you and giving you hope?

3. How has the Lord strengthened you for your work as a mother? Try to list one specific example for each of the previous months.

4. Read 1 Samuel 1:21-28, and write out verses 26-28.

5. Hannah recognized that Samuel was a gift, and that she therefore needed to dedicate him to the Lord. Have you truly acknowledged that your child is a gift you cannot possess?

6. a. Just as the physical weaning is ideally a gradual event, so is emotional weaning. When Hannah says that Samuel "will be given over to the LORD" (verse 28), her words connote a process, a daily giving over of the child to the Lord. How have you given over your child to the Lord thus far?

    b. Are there areas you are still clinging to and possessing regarding your child?

    c. Write out how you can prepare for your child's release into the world even at this early stage.

7. a. Read Psalm 139:13-16. Write down the verbs in verses 13, 15, and 16.

    b. These verbs clarify God's activity in creating your child. Since the Lord formed your child, He knows him or her more intimately than you do. Recognizing this crucial point will enable you to shape your child's character according to the Lord's design, not your own. Ask God to show you any areas in which you have imposed your design on your child, instead of His. Write down what He reveals to you.

8. a. Read Psalm 144:12, and write it out below.

    b. Meditate on this verse, and write down what it means to you as you consider your son or daughter.

    c. How can you begin now to ensure the fulfillment of this verse?

9. a. Read Psalm 131, and write out verse 2.

b. As you meditate on this psalm, what is your child's disposition in your arms?

c. Now think of yourself as being in your heavenly Father's arms.

How are you like the psalm describes?

How are you like your child in your arms?

10. As you thank the Father for His constant presence with you this first year, and as you give Him the next milestone ahead, ask Him to show you where your soul is not at rest in your role as a mother. Write down what He reveals to you.

─────────────── | PRAYERS AND ANSWERS | ───────────────

Rejoice and give thanks for God's care and grace through your first year of mothering.

Specifically give thanks for the answers you have received to prayers you recorded in this book.

Ask God to show you how to encourage the development of your child's individual character.

Pray for the ability to entrust your child fully into God's hands.

Pray for mothers you know who are expecting their first child. Ask God to show you how you can be His vessel of encouragement during their first year.

As you complete the celebration of your first birthday as a mother, I leave you with a challenge for the many milestones awaiting you. Continue to record your personal growth and development as a mother. Take time either weekly or monthly to reflect on the changes and struggles you are encountering. Write them out, along with your prayers. You may want to also jot down how your child is becoming his or her own person.

This personal record will be invaluable to you many years from now. You will see how your child has blossomed into a unique person and how the Lord Jesus has made you more like Him through His calling for you—a mother.

"Is your God an all-wise Father, who knows the end from the beginning, who knows all the causes and all the outcomes, and who never makes a mistake?. . . This view of God as an omniscient Father comes into focus very clearly as the years pass. One of the advantages of growing older is that we can look back and see that God has not made a single mistake in our lives. . . . It's exciting to recognize as the years come and go that everything has worked together for good if we have really loved Him."

Evelyn Christenson
What Happens When Women Pray

NOTES:
1. Charles R. Swindoll, *You and Your Child* (Fullerton, Calif.: Insight for Living, 1986), page 53.
2. Swindoll, *You and Your Child*, page 49.
3. Used by permission from Sandra B. Clark. Her article "Can My Love Protect My Child?" appeared in the May/June 1985 issue of *Today's Christian Woman*.

For those of us who dwell on large land masses, the shore is often the end of a journey, but also a new frontier; it presents a boundary, but a clean view of the horizon as well.

Luci Shaw
Postcard from the Shore

We have come to the end of our "beach walk" together. The completion of one year of motherhood is a boundary at which we can stand and look at the horizon, the future ahead for us and our children.

We will miss walking and talking with you because we have come to think of you as our friends. Thank you for "listening" to some of our experiences and thoughts, and for exploring our ideas for yourself.

We will pray for you as your journey continues on a new frontier. Jesus Christ walks with you, and because of Him, the journey will go on in joy.

BIBLIOGRAPHY

Allen, Ronald and Beverly. *Liberated Traditionalism*. Portland, Oreg.: Multnomah Press, 1985.

Anderson, Ray and Dennis B. Guernsey. *On Being Family: A Social Theology of the Family*. Grand Rapids: Eerdmans, 1985.

"'Baby bust' threatens to change American society." *The Atlanta Journal and Constitution*. July 5, 1987, Section C, page 1C.

Bence, Evelyn. *Leaving Home*. Philadelphia, Penn.: Westminster Press, 1952.

Berg, Barbara T. *The Crisis of the Working Mother*. New York: Simon and Schuster, 1986.

Black, Patsie. *Tapestry: A Finespun Grace and Mercy*. Portland, Oreg.: Multnomah Press, 1982.

Burtchaell, James T. "In a Family Way." *Christianity Today*. June 12, 1987, pages 24-27.

Callahan, Sidney Cornelia. *The Illusion of Eve: Modern Woman's Quest for Identity*. New York: Sheed and Ward, 1965.

Caplan, Frank and Theresa. *The Power of Play*. New York:

Anchor Press/Doubleday, 1973.

Christenson, Evelyn. *What Happens When Women Pray?* Wheaton, Ill.: Scripture Press Publications, 1980.

Clark, Sandra B. "Can My Love Protect My Child?" *Today's Christian Woman.* May/June 1985.

Davidson, R. *Genesis 1-11: The Cambridge Bible Commentary on the New English Bible.* Cambridge, Great Britain: Cambridge University Press, 1973.

Deutsch, Helene. *The Psychology of Women, Volume II— Motherhood.* New York: Bantam Books, 1945.

Evans, Colleen and Louis, Jr. *Bold Commitment.* Wheaton, Ill.: Scripture Press Publications, 1983.

Fallows, Deborah. *A Mother's Work.* Boston: Houghton Mifflin Company, 1985.

Fischer, Lucy Rose, Ph.D. *Linked Lives.* New York: Harper & Row, 1986.

Fleming, Jean. *Between Walden and the Whirlwind.* Colorado Springs, Colo.: NavPress, 1985.

Fraiberg, Selma. *Every Child's Birthright.* New York: Basic Books, 1977.

Gansberg, Judith and Arthur J. Mostel, M.D. *The Second Nine Months: The Sexual and Emotional Concerns of the New Mother.* New York: Tribeca, 1984.

Genevie, Louis and Eva Margolies, eds. *The Motherhood Report.* New York: Macmillan, 1987.

Hulme, William. *Firstborn.* St. Louis: Concordia, 1972.

Insel, Deborah. *Motherhood: Your First Twelve Months.* Washington, D.C.: Acropolis Books, Ltd., 1982.

Jepsen, Dee. *Women: Beyond Equal Rights.* Waco, Tex.: Word Books, 1984.

Johnston, Jon. "Growing Me-ism and Materialism." *Christianity Today.* January 17, 1986, pages 16-I, 17-I.

Julian of Norwich. *Revelations of Divine Love.* England: Penguin Books, 1966.

Kitzinger, Sheila. *Women as Mothers: How They See Themselves in Different Cultures.* New York: Random House, 1978.

Kuykendall, Carol. *Learning to Let Go.* Grand Rapids: Zondervan Publishing House, 1985.

Lewis, C.S. *The Great Divorce.* New York: Macmillan Publishing Co., Inc., 1946.

Mason, Mike. *The Mystery of Marriage.* Portland, Oreg.: Multnomah Press, 1985.

Morris, Leon. *The Gospel According to John.* Grand Rapids: Eerdmans, 1971.

Neale, Robert E. *In Praise of Play: Toward a Psychology of Religion.* New York: Harper & Row, 1969.

Nouwen, Henri. *Making All Things New.* San Francisco: Harper & Row, 1981.

Ogilvie, Lloyd John. *The Beauty of Friendship.* Irvine, Calif.: Harvest House Publishers, 1980.

Olds, Sally, Marcia London, P.A. Ladewig, and Sharon Davidson. *Obstetric Nursing.* Menlo Park, Calif.: Addison-Wesley Publishing Co., 1980.

Pape, Dorothy R. *In Search of God's Ideal Woman.* Downers Grove, Ill.: InterVarsity Press, 1976.

Piers, Maria W. and Genevieve Millet Landau. *The Gift of Play: And Why Young Children Cannot Thrive Without It.* New York: Walker and Co., 1980.

Quindlen, Ann. "Baby Craving." *Life.* June 1987, pages 23-26.

Rabrizzi, Kathryn. *The Sacred and the Feminine: Toward a Theology of Housework.* New York: Seabury Press, 1982.

Rubin, Nancy. *The Mother Mirror.* New York: Putnam's Sons, 1984.

Sandford, John and Paula. *The Transformation of the Inner Man.* Tulsa, Okla.: Victory House, Inc., 1982.

Shaw, Luci. *Postcard from the Shore.* Wheaton, Ill.: Harold Shaw Publishers, 1985.

Shreve, Anita. *Remaking Motherhood.* New York: Viking Penguin, Inc., 1986.

Stedman, Elaine. *A Woman's Worth.* Waco, Tex.: Word Books, 1980.

Swindoll, Charles R. *You and Your Child.* Fullerton, Calif.: Insight for Living, 1986.

"Three's a Crowd." *Newsweek.* September 1, 1986, pages 68-76.

Urbanska, Wanda. *The Singular Generation.* Garden City, N.Y.: Doubleday, 1986.

Walsh, Huber M. and Shirley K. "Your Values as a Parent." *The First Years of Parenting.* Crawfordsville, Ind.: Presbyterian Church in the United States, 1979.

Washbourn, Penelope. *Becoming Woman: The Quest for Wholeness in Female Experience.* San Francisco: Harper & Row, 1977.